Roger, Sausage & Whippet

Roger, Sausage & Whippet

A Miscellany of Trench Lingo from The Great War

Christopher Moore

headline

First published in 2012
by HEADLINE PUBLISHING GROUP

1

Cataloguing in Publication Data is available from the British Library

Hardback ISBN 978 0 7553 6367 4

Typeset in ITC Cheltenham by Avon DataSet Ltd,
Bidford-on-Avon, Warwickshire

Printed and bound in Great Britain by Clays Ltd, St Ives plc

Designed by Lynnette Eve/www.design-jam.co.uk

Cigarette Card images © Imperial Tobacco Group Plc

Headline's policy is to use papers that are natural, renewable and
recyclable products and made from wood grown in sustainable forests.
The logging and manufacturing processes are expected to conform to the
environmental regulations of the country of origin.

HEADLINE PUBLISHING GROUP
An Hachette UK Company
338 Euston Road
London NW1 3BH

www.headline.co.uk
www.hachette.co.uk

To
Walter Butterworth,
Private,
1/5th Battallion the Leicestershire Regiment, T.F.,
France & Flanders, 1915–1918.
He talked the talk.

My dear Daphne,

Thank you so much for your recent charming and gossipful
letter. Yes is the answer to your question, I did know
they had kept our letters from the war -- but I had quite
forgotten the trench lingo we used to spice them up.

Your dear old pa didn't know what we were talking about
half the time. Just before I went to France in 1915 he asked
me for a glossary. I wrote six or seven of them during the
course of the war, and your uncle Jack wrote a couple too,
after he joined the Navy. When I was in hospital with my leg
your pa suggested that writing up my little word-books might
help to pass the time. I had them bound by the stationer
in Tonbridge who used to print our letter-heads. One copy
went to Fudge for the Etchingham library - he had it re-
bound, of course, with the family crest - another went to my
regimental Old Comrades' Association.

We had some great laughs as well as our dole of tragedy.
Alternatively, if you really are spending a while at the old
place, I could motor up, perhaps next weekend, if McCarthy
gets over his sciatica by then and can drive again. There
are one or two things I might be interested in before the
auctioneer gets his hands on them - for example, that nice
landscape hanging in Mudge's upstairs sitting room. I'm sure I
could find a space for it.

Ever your loving uncle,

Charles Cartwright
(Captain!)

IS FOR

ARMY

'C' Company, 5th West Kent Fusiliers,
British Expeditionary Force,
15th June, 1915.

Dear Mudge and Fudge,

Here we are at last – <u>Somewhere in France</u>
– and how childishly thrilling it is. The crossing
from Southampton was tolerable despite our being
crammed into a rusty old Irish cattle transport
with the absolute minimum of amenities, by which
I mean dirty straw below decks for the men and
a single cabin for the six officers of 'C' Coy. At
least none of <u>Jerry's tin fish</u> sought to interfere
with our moonlit passage. I am not allowed to
tell you where we landed, although you know it well
from days of yore. Nor had the holiday spirit quite
departed from the place, despite the preponderance
of <u>khaki.</u> One might think the <u>Froggies</u> ought to
be growing tired of <u>Tommy</u> by now but there was
a modest quantity of cheering as we marched up
the hill, followed by urchins begging for <u>biskwee</u>
and <u>bull-ee</u> and choco-la every step of the way.
The <u>C.O.</u> got ahead of us on his <u>charger</u> and was
waiting at our allotted <u>hutment.</u> 'You men,' he
announced, chewing fiercely on his moustache,
'are West Kent Fusiliers. You are serving in
one of the best <u>regiments</u> in the best <u>Army</u> in
the world. Having watched your progress closely

during training, I have formed a high opinion of your capabilities. Now that we face the real enemy I expect you to do your duty to the utmost and, when the moment comes, to fight like hell and die like Englishmen. You are a <u>bloody</u> fine <u>mob</u> and I am proud to command you. Dismiss!" It almost made me feel the Army was not such an awful old Moloch after all.

I am writing in haste to catch the post. Let me know how long this takes to reach you. The address above is my postal abode in the Army until further notice, nothing else is needed.

With love to everyone at home,
   your warrior son,

Charles

A.A.A. The code for a full stop in an Army message. Colloquially, a hint to a comrade to stop talking rubbish. See also, **Signalese**.

Abdullas. Cigarettes for officers made from Turkish or Egyptian tobacco. Anyone in the ranks in receipt of a **buckshee** Abdulla would seek to swap it for something less luxurious, despite an unfavourable rate of exchange.

Accessory. The Army code word for the gas released at Loos, 25 September 1915. Six thousand canisters of **chlorine** were **humped** into the **trenches** to precede the **infantry** assault; much of it failed to reach **Jerry**'s lines.

Ace. A pilot with more than five confirmed kills to his credit. The first ace was a Frenchman, Adolphe Pégoud, killed 31 August 1915. The highest-scoring ace was the German Manfred von Richthofen, the Red Baron, with 80 kills. The highest-scoring English ace was Mick Mannock, with 73 kills. **Jerry** also awarded the term to submarine commanders. From the French, *as*, ace in a suit of cards.

Ack Emma. The letters A and M in **Signalese**, the alphabetic language of British military signallers. Ack Emma = A.M. = morning.

Adjutant. The executive officer of any unit, responsible for admin, paperwork and communications. In an **infantry battalion**, he was the colonel's right-hand man but not his second-in-command. Officers were entitled to abbreviate adjutant to Adj, which could also be used as a verb, as in 'The **Old Man**'s asked if I'll adj for him when Smithy goes on leave.' From the Latin *juvare*, to assist.

Adrian helmet. The French **tin lid**, named after the general who invented it. Also known as *casserole*, oven dish, and *pot de chambre*. See also, **Battle bowler**.

A.E.F. The American Expeditionary Force sent to Europe by the United States after it entered the war on the **Allied** side, 6 April 1917. The initials A.E.F. were also said to stand for 'After England Failed'. See also, **Doughboy**, **Yank**.

Afters. The Army word for pudding. Colloquially, an extra helping of anything bad.

'Aim it at the Germans!' Reproof for anyone inadvertently pointing a weapon where he should not.

Air cavalry. A derisive, faintly jealous **infantry** term for the **Royal Flying Corps**, **R.F.C.** The phrase conveys the early military thinking that aircraft would be most useful in war for reconnaissance.

Aldershot. The home garrison and headquarters of the British Army, usually abbreviated to the Shot.

'All dressed up like a Christmas tree!' The description of an **infantry private** in full marching order with his accoutrements hanging off his **webbing**.

Alleyman. A German, the enemy. **Tommy**'s French. From *Allemand*, a German. See also, **Boche**, **Fritz**, **Hun**, **Jerry**.

'Alley! Alley toot sweet! Alley at the toot!' Scarper! Get out quick! **Tommy**'s French. From '*Allez tout de suite!*', go at once.

Ally Sloper's Cavalry. The Army Service Corps (. responsible for supply and transport. Also known as Corps or more politely, the **Ascots**. At the start of the drivers were regarded as skilled workers. They received a day at a time when the infantryman was getting a basic ...ng. *Ally Sloper's Half Holiday* was an illustrated comic for adults, Ally Sloper himself being a red-nosed scrounger whose escapades often ended with him getting away with it by sloping off down some convenient alley.

Ally, Allies. A friendly country in the war, those alongside whom it was being fought. On the **Western Front**, these were France and Belgium, later the Portuguese and the Americans. On the Eastern Front, the ally was Russia, in the south it was Italy. Ally was an officer's word. **Tommy** called his foreign comrades by their proper names, **Froggie**, **Belgie**, **Yank** and **Ivan**. See also, **Central Powers**.

'Am I hurting you? I should be, I'm standing on your hair! What are you – some kind of *woman*!?' An N.C.O.'s witticism, shouted on **parade** while standing right behind any man whose hair touched the top of his ears or his collar. See also, **'Get your ears put back!'**

Ameens. Tommy's French. The city of Amiens.

Amen snorter, amen wallah. See **Padre**.

Ammo. Ammunition. See also, **Limber**, **Round**.

Angel's whisper. The bugle call summoning **defaulters**. See also, **Jankers men**.

Anglische. What the average **Belgie** spoke to a **Tommy** in response to his **Frahnsay**.

'Any complaints?' A strictly rhetorical question from an officer when visiting his men after a meal. Should any complaint be forthcoming it would be met with unpleasant retaliation from a **babbler** or **quartermaster**. The phrase was also used as a conversational gambit when two soldiers met.

'Any more for any more?' A **babbler**'s shout, offering second helpings. Also, in the game of **Crown and Anchor**, it was the announcement that betting was about to close.

ANZAC. Literally, Australia & New Zealand Army Corps. The ANZACs started arriving on the **Western Front** from Gallipoli in 1916. Newspapers applied the acronym to any Australian or New Zealand soldier; **Tommy** preferred **Aussie**.

'Apree la gar . . .' A phrase meaning some time in the vague future, whenever, perhaps never. **Tommy**'s French. From *après la guerre fini*, after the war is over.

Archie, Archibald. Anti-aircraft defences. Archie might refer to an anti-aircraft gun, the shells it fired or a member of its crew. Black Archie was German anti-aircraft fire, from the colour of its burst. British Archie was white. To be archied was to be hit by such fire. From a popular song in which a young lady evaded her suitor's overenthusiastic advances with the phrase, 'Archibald, certainly not!' See also, *Flak*.

Armful. An Army measurement of volume which was larger than a couple-of-handfuls and about the same as a bucket-load. A woman judged to be a nice armful was of buxom proportions.

Armin, Arm-in-arm. The French town of Armentieres, close to the Belgian border. One of its daughters was made famous in a lewd marching song. In 1915 Armin was so quiet and pleasant some regiments referred to it as the Peace Sector. There were excellent cafés and pastry shops and a handy branch of **Burberry's**.

Army. The largest military formation deployed by the **British Expeditionary Force, B.E.F.** When an **infantry battalion** was in

rest, it was one of the **subaltern**'s duties, on clement afternoons when there was no more pressing occupation for the men, to instruct them with an improving lecture. A list of recommended themes was maintained by the **adjutant**. One of them was known as *The Chain of Command*. The official British chain of command started with the Prime Minister and his cabinet. They were answerable for the conduct of the war to the British people through their sovereign Parliament. Over the road from Downing Street was the War Office, seat of the Minister for War, Lord **Kitchener**. His duty was to advise the government on military matters and to formulate strategies in line with their political objectives. Quiet at the back. Each of the five armies in the **B.E.F.** was commanded by a full general in rank, who answered to the Commander-in-Chief, **C-in-C**, at **G.H.Q.**, **General Headquarters.** Each army consisted of a number of corps, three to five of them, commanded by a lieutenant-general with his own headquarters of staff officers. Each corps consisted of two or three **infantry divisions** commanded by a major-general. Each infantry division consisted of three **brigades** commanded by a **brigadier**. Each brigade consisted of four infantry **battalions**, commanded by a lieutenant-colonel. Each battalion consisted of four **companies** of men, commanded by a **captain**, with a **sergeant-major** to assist. Each company consisted of four **platoons**, commanded by a **lieutenant** or second lieutenant, with a **sergeant** to assist. Each platoon consisted of sections, under a **corporal** or **lance jack**. The average **private** cared about none of it. All he cared about was his **mob** – the **muckers** in his platoon with whom he shared his privations and faced the enemy, shoulder to shoulder. **Tommy**'s home in the Army was his **regiment** and that was all he cared about. Everything else, including the chain of command, was **bull**.

Army language. Swearing, conversational profanity. See also, **Language**.

Arrival. A colloquial expression for a shell bursting in British lines.

Arsty! Slow down! Go slow. From the Hindustani *ahisti*. The opposite of **jildy**.

Artificer. Army jargon for a skilled mechanic, especially one employed in the maintenance and repair of weapons. From the Latin *artificium*, to make artfully.

WILLS'S CIGARETTES.

FIELD-MARSHAL SIR D. HAIG.

Artillery. The **guns**. The tactics of both sides for much of the war was summed up in the phrase, 'Artillery conquers, **infantry** occupies.' From the Old French *artiller*, to equip. See also, **Royal Artillery**, **Royal Horse Artillery**.

Artists' Rifles. The 28th Battalion, London Regiment, famous for the large number of artists, writers, musicians and actors who served in it and took commissions. At one point it was said to be providing the Army with 100 **subalterns** per month.

A.S.C. See **Ally Sloper's Cavalry**.

Ascots. Army Service Corps. See also, **Ally Sloper's Cavalry**.

Asquiths. French-made matches. Once struck, smokers had to wait and see if they caught flame. Named after the wait and see policies of H. H. Asquith, the Liberal Prime Minister at the start of the war, notorious for his steadfast indecision. Asquith's eldest son, Raymond, was killed 15 September 1916.

Attached roof. A luxury in **billets**.

Attrition. The military strategy whereby each side seeks victory by wearing down the other through the mutual expenditure of men and material. The German word was *materialschlacht*, battle of material. The French **C-in-C**, Papa Joffre, was an exponent of attritional warfare: 'It is the final **battalions** that bring victory.' From the Latin *terere*, to rub.

Aussie. An Australian. The Aussies and **Canucks** were better paid than **Tommy** and resented by him for pushing up prices in **estaminys**. See also, **ANZAC**, **Digger**.

A.W.O.L. Absent Without Official Leave, a military crime. Pronounced as a set of initials not as the word awol.

Axle grease. Butter. A rare treat in **trenches**. In German, *wagenschmiere*, axle grease, or *Kaiser-Wilhelm-Deichtnis-Schmiere*, Kaiser Wilhelm Memorial Spread.

Ayrton fan. Device for dispersing **Jerry**'s gas. It was a flap of canvas attached to a broomstick. When gas fumes were thick on the ground, the Ayrton fan was used to sweep them aside. Named after its inventor, Mrs Hertha Ayrton, who paid for 150,000 of them to be sent to France, where many ended up as firewood.

B

IS FOR

BLOODY

'C' Company, 5th West Kent Fusiliers,
British Expeditionary Force,
26th June, 1915.

Dear Edward,

Yes, you can share the contents of my letters
with whomsoever, at your discretion. You can
tell my darling nephews & kneesers that I will be
writing to them separately but only if they write
to me first. I am becoming ruthless at collecting
correspondents. Letters are an absolute lifeline
out here. They need be neither informative nor
entertaining, mere contact is what counts . . .
Today we are moving up the Line, but with no
great velocity. We were roused at three ack emma
and marched to the railhead by seven. We then had
to wait two hours for the train, standing out in
the pouring rain like dumb beasts. Since then
we've been heading Front-wards at a maximum
ten miles per hour with the clothes drying slowly
on our backs . . . We 'C' Coy subalterns have
made ourselves as cushy as poss by spreading our
valises on the filthed upholstery while our men are
crammed next door in a hom forty. 'Bloody hell!' I
hear, 'That's a bad cough you've got there. Can't
you smother it!' There is no glass in our windows
so all the backchat comes straight through. 'Do you
know, Stan,' came the reply, 'that bugger of an

<u>M.O.</u>, he wouldn't look at me this morning. Called me a bloody shirker and here I am barking like a pregnant cow.'

The constant swearing irritates some of my fellow officers but we all do it, except in the <u>mess.</u> Only senior officers are allowed to let rip in the mess, and only then if the <u>Old Man</u> leads the way, which he often does. Poor old Mudge would be appalled to hear us carrying on. Bugger and bloody pass as chaff. One hears more of f--- and c--- in one hour out here than in a whole year at home. This war has some terrors in store for us for sure but I cannot help thinking that, against the worst it can show, our <u>lingo</u> is pure innocence.

Trusting this finds you <u>in the pink</u>,
your brother,

Chaz

Babbler. A cook. From rhyming slang, babbling brook.

Backchat. Good-humoured argument or raillery. From the Hindustani *batchit*.

Back curtain. The backdrop to a **show** or **stunt**, a **barrage** of artillery fire laid down behind **Jerry**'s line to prevent him bringing up reinforcements.

Bale out. To jump to safety with a parachute. Baling out was only possible for **observers** in **sausages**. Pilots and observers in aeroplanes were not so equipped. It was felt that the opportunity of escape offered by the **brolly** might corrode the martial spirit.

Ballistite. An explosive invented by Alfred Nobel for cartridges. From the Latin *ballista*, a siege engine for hurling rocks. The British refused to recognise Nobel's patent and synthesised ballistite under the name **cordite**.

Balloon, observation. See **Sausage**.

Balloon bed. The place where **sausages** were tethered for the night.

Balloon buster. A pilot expert at destroying **sausages**. This was more difficult than it might seem. For one thing, **Jerry** always defended them with **Archie** or **flaming onions**. For another, when a sausage was hit by **tracer** its hydrogen gas was meant to ignite, which could burn the attacking plane as it passed.

Balloonatic. Member of a balloon unit. Also, a synonym for **balloon buster**.

Bangalore torpedo. A length of sheet steel folded like a drainpipe and stuffed with explosive to blow a path through **Jerry**'s barbed wire. Each torpedo would be carried across **No Man's Land** under cover of darkness and slid into position to await detonation. Named after the **sappers'** depot in Bangalore, India, where the device was first made.

Banjo. A shovel. Australian derivation.

Bantam, banty. A short soldier. From the word for a dwarf fowl. In 1914 the Army's minimum recruiting height was 5ft 3ins. In 1915 the Cheshire Regiment became the first to recruit men below this height and in 1916 the requirement for bantams was officially set between 5ft 1in and 5ft 4ins. At one point there was an entire **division** of bantams – the 35th Division – but by the end of 1916 the fitness of **sawn-off** volunteers was in decline and the scheme was abandoned.

WILLS'S CIGARETTES.

A TRIBUTE TO THE ROYAL ENGINEERS

Barbed wire, on the. Location unknown. When a unit mustered for roll call after an attack, 'hanging on the wire' meant of any absent comrade, killed. The phrase was also used conversationally: 'Where's my **bloody** soap gone?' 'Hanging on the wire.'

Barber's Cat. A gossip or chatterbox.

Barrage. Artillery fire so concentrated as to provide a curtain or wall of explosions. From the French *barrer*, to bar. A **creeping barrage** was a wall of shell-fire that moved forward by a series of co-ordinated lifts at regular intervals. The timing and distance of each lift determined the speed of the attack. If the **infantry** stuck too closely to their creeping barrage, they risked being hit. If they didn't stick closely enough, they gave the enemy time to rally once the barrage had lifted over them. The creeping barrage was a proven way to break into enemy **trenches** but the extent of such penetration was limited by the range of the guns that made it possible.

Base. A French town given over to the supply needs of the British Army. As the war progressed, bases grew up near all the Channel ports. The largest was at Etaples, which had Boulogne as its feeder port. See also, **Eat Apples**.

Basher. A **P.T.** instructor. See also, **Bull ring**, **Canary**.

Basket case. A **casualty** with no legs or arms. In French, *cul-de-jatte*, basin-arse.

Bat, sling the. To sling the bat was to talk the language of the native population. From the Hindustani *bat*, language. To parlay the bat in France was to speak **Frahnsay**. Bat was also an abbreviation for a **batman**.

Batman. An officer's personal servant, responsible for his creature comforts in the field. French derivation, from *bat*, an officer's pack horse, the soldier in charge of which was a batman. The verb was to bat, as in, 'If you're looking for a **cushy** number, that new officer **bloke** is looking for someone to bat for him.'

Battalion, batt. The largest constituent unit of a British **infantry regiment**. Each full-strength battalion consisted of about one thousand men, led by a lieutenant-colonel. Some county regiments raised thirty or more battalions during the war. From the French and German *bataillon*.

Battle bowler. The British steel helmet, patented in August 1915 by John Brodie and issued at **trench stores** in October of that year. Made from manganese steel, it was said to be twice as hard as the French **Adrian helmet**. See also, *Stalhelm*, **Tin lid**.

Battle casualty. See Casualty.

Battye bomb. A hand grenade improvised in time for the Battle of Loos, 25 September 1915. The fuse was inserted by hand and fired by a patent lighter. It was not a popular weapon.

Bayonet. The long dagger attached to the end of a rifle to enable it as a stabbing weapon. Reputedly derived from the French town of Bayonne, where daggers were made. See also, **Candlestick**, **Rosalie**, **Sword**, **Toasting fork**.

Beak, boko. See **Conk**.

Beano. A feast or spree, often celebrating the award of a **gong** or a promotion.

Beetle crusher. An infantryman.

Beetle crushers. An infantryman's boots, his **daisies**.

B.E.F. See **British Expeditionary Force**.

Belgie. A Belgian. From which came the adjective Belgique, meaning odd, different, not quite right. **Tommy** considered it highly Belgique, for example, that the Belgian army used dogs instead of men for pulling machine-gun carts.

Bellyache. A serious wound in the stomach, usually fatal.

Big Bertha. Generic nickname for any long-range **Jerry** gun. From Bertha Krupp, heiress to the industrial dynasty which owned Germany's biggest manufacturer of munitions.

Big noise. An important person. In French, *gros légume*, big vegetable.

Big Willie. The German **Kaiser**, Wilhelm II. From a series of *Daily Mirror* cartoons of him and his son, the Crown Prince, **Little Willie**.

Billet. A civilian dwelling or outhouse commandeered for the accommodation of troops. Also, the actual **chit (1)** requiring civilians to offer up their hospitality to the Army. From Old French *billette*, a note.

Billy Wells. Heavy artillery. From Bombardier Billy Wells, a champion heavyweight boxer who served in the Army as a **basher**.

Bing Boys, Bing Bangs. Literally, *The Bing Boys* was a musical revue playing at the Alhambra Theatre in London, 1916–18. It was most famous for the song 'If You Were The Only Girl In The World'. Colloquially, the name was applied to any group of cheerful comrades. See also, **Byng Boys**.

Bingo. The only form of gambling tolerated in the Army.

Bint. Sexually mature young woman, possibly available, not necessarily a prostitute. From the Arabic for girl.

Biscuits. Small, hard military mattresses, three to a bed.

Biskwee. Tommy's French. From *bisquit*, a biscuit, i.e. **hard tack**.

Black as the ace of spades. An approved Army simile for blank darkness.

Black as the inside of a cow. Very dark indeed.

Black hand gang. Men chosen and equipped for a hazardous patrol or trench raid. From the Serbian anarchist group the Black Hand, responsible for the assassination in 1914 of the Austrian Archduke Franz Ferdinand, this act precipitated the war.

Blanket drill. Sleep, especially an afternoon snooze. Also, to masturbate (under the covers).

Blighty. England. Home. From the Urdu *bilaiti*, province. A blighty one was a wound requiring evacuation to England; in German, *heimatschuss*, a home-shot; in French, *fine blessure*, a fine wound. All meant the same to the man who had one – clean sheets and safety.

Blind. A **dud**, a shell failing to explode. Also, a drinking spree.

Blind pig. A German mortar bomb. See also, **Minnie**, **Sausage**.

Blink. A nicked-off **fag** saved for later enjoyment.

Blinker. Generic for signalling lamp. Also, the man operating it.

Bloke. A man, the basic unit of military manpower. Bloke was also applied as a suffix in the same way as *wallah*. The post bloke was the man sent to fetch the mail. An officer's bloke was his **batman**.

Bloody. The commonest Army swear word, along with **bugger**. See **Ruddy**.

Blow the gaff. To disclose a secret. See **Gaff**.

Blue, the. Out of contact. A patrol was said to have gone into the blue when it had no reliable way of getting messages back and there was no support on either side. The opposite was out of the blue – to arrive without notice or warning.

Blue Lamp. A brothel for officers, from the light used to advertise its services. See **Red Lamp**.

Bob-down man. A **sentry** whose job was to warn of approaching enemy aircraft whereupon everyone had to **bob** down, i.e. take cover. Men were ordered never to look up when a **Jerry** plane was over the lines, since a row of upturned faces in a **trench** revealed instantly that it was occupied and might be worth an **artillery salvo**.

Bob. The correct verb for ducking one's head for the purpose of self-preservation.

Bobbajee. A cook. From the Hindustani *bawachi*, cook. See also, **Babbler**.

Bobber. One who **bobbed** too much, a symptom of being **windy**.

Bobbing on it. Awaiting something unpleasant. A man who was bobbing on his next mail was expecting bad news in a letter. See also, **Sweating on it**.

Boche, Bosches. A German, the Germans. From French slang. The

Germans regarded Boche as an offensive epithet unlike **Fritz** or **Jerry**. See also, **Hun**.

Bodysnatcher. A **sniper** or **stretcher bearer**.

Bomb. A hand grenade. From the French *bombe*. See also, **Mills bomb**, **Potato masher**.

Bomb proof. Adjective for a **dug-out** or post that had been strengthened to withstand attack from hand grenades but not shells or aircraft **eggs**.

Bon, bong. A term of approbation. **Tommy**'s French. From *bon*, good. A bon tom was a good time, *bon temps*. Bon sonty was a toast to good health, *bonne santé*. The opposite of bon was not the French *mal* but no bon. As in, *Bong soir, Mamzel. Combien? No bon*, which translates as 'Good evening, Miss. How much? Not likely'.

Booka. Hungry. From the Hindustani *bhukha*, hungry.

Boozilier. A **fusilier** skilled in alcoholic consumption. See also, **Methusilier**.

Bowler hat, order of. To be sacked from command was to be awarded the Order of the Bowler Hat and returned to **Civvy Street**. Officers' figure of speech.

Box. Coffin.

Box of tricks. The mechanical part of a weapon that made it useful or lethal, for example the fuse or detonating device of a **bomb**.

Brad, brads. Pound notes. Until the war, the only British banknote was for the value of five pounds but on Friday, 7 August 1914 the first pound note appeared, printed in a hurry on the same paper used for postage stamps and signed by the Permanent Secretary to the Treasury, Sir John Bradbury.

Brass. The correct collective noun for senior officers. See also, **Red tab**.

Brass hat. A senior officer. From the quantity of braid on his cap.

Breezer. A rest. As in, 'Give us a breezer, **Corp**. We're **buggered**.'

Brevet. A promotion in an officer's rank without an increase in pay. Promotion in the Army was earned by **Buggins' turn**. The award of a brevet rank gave the holder the right to jump the queue the next time promotion came round.

Brew. Tea. To make a cup of tea was to brew up. See also, **Drum up, Makings**.

Brigade. A British **infantry** brigade (for most of the war) consisted of four **battalions** and its **artillery**. A brigade was commanded by a brigadier-general, also known as a **brigadier**. Chief of the brigadier's staff was the brigade major, who was responsible for the fighting fitness, training and Intelligence of the **P.B.I.** The brigade's **staff captain** was responsible for its stores, supplies and administration. See also, **Brass hat, Red tab**.

British Expeditionary Force, B.E.F. The force sent by the Army to France in August 1914. It comprised about 120,000 men. By the time of the Armistice, 1918, the B.E.F. numbered about 3,000,000 men.

British Summer Time. The first time the clocks in England went forward in summer was in May 1916. See also, **Dora**.

Broke, to be. To lose one's **stripes**, to be demoted. The approved verb for the process of returning an **N.C.O.** to the ranks to punish him for a **crime**.

Brolly. Parachute. **Civvy** slang for umbrella. See also, **Bale out**.

Bromide. A compound allegedly put into **char** to curtail the sexual urges. See also, **Jollop**.

Bubbly. A look-out. During illicit games of chance, it was the bubbly's job to warn of an approaching **N.C.O.** or officer. See also, **Crown and Anchor**.

Buckshee. Free, a gift. From the Arabic *baksheesh*, alms. The Buckshee King was the paymaster. He travelled from unit to unit, issuing pay and accounting for it.

Bugger. A ubiquitous noun and verb. Any man or thing could be referred to as a bugger and subjected to an endless variety of buggering about. As a vice, buggery was attributed to the Royal Navy. A soldier reprimanded for saying bugger could defend himself by explaining it was a term of endearment among **matlows**.

Buggins' turn. The Army system of promoting by order of seniority.

Bull, bullshit. The Army way of doing things, with maximum jargon from the officers and the minimum of consideration for the **Other Ranks**.

Bull ring. The central training ground at the huge **base** camp at **Eat Apples**. The term was extended to similar training grounds at **depots** across France.

Bully beef, bully. Cooked beef in a can. See also, **Fray Bentos**.

Bully gas. The foul stink, also known as canned gangrene, that sometimes hissed out when a tin of rotten **bully** was opened.

Bully in disguise. Corned beef mixed with other ingredients. Biscuit crumbs, chopped onions, etc. were often added to make **bully** into stew, hash or rissoles.

Bumf. Any Army form or document emanating from the military bureaucracy. From bum fodder, paper for wiping purposes. See also, **Chit (1)**.

Bumface. General Sir Hubert Gough, unlucky commander of the Fifth Army when **Jerry** smashed it in March 1918. From the crevice in his somewhat bulbous nose.

Bunce. A small bribe in cash or kind, something for nothing.

Bung. Cheese.

Bungo. General Sir Julian Byng. See **Byng Boys**.

Burberry. A brand of waterproof trench coat for officers. Burberry was also the recognised English pronunciation of the French town of Burbure.

Burgoo. Porridge.

Burst. A volley of fire from a machine gun. A man hit by the first **round** from a burst could be hit again ten times before reaching the ground. See also, **Hose**, **Squirt**.

Bus. Aeroplane. A pilot's term of affection.

Butcher. The battalion **M.O.**, **Medical Officer**. Also, a surgeon. Also, any commander perceived to be impervious to **casualties**.

Butt. The wooden stock of one's **hipe**. There was a little compartment inside for storing a brass phial of oil for cleaning the inside of the barrel. See also, **Lee Enfield**.

Butt notcher. A **sniper**. From his practice of marking each *coup* with a notch on his rifle's butt.

Buzz. A rumour or **signal** leading to sudden activity. Among **signallers**, to buzz was to send a message on a buzzer, a field telegraph or telephone which was carried in a stout leather case on a shoulder strap and transmitted messages in **Morse code** down a buzz wire. Buzzers in forward **trenches** were connected to **Battalion** HQ which was connected to **Brigade**. It was part of a signaller's job to keep these wires repaired. A signaller operating a buzzer was also called a buzzer. See also, **Signalese**.

Byng Boys. Canadians. More than 418,000 of them served on the **Western Front**. More than half became **casualties**. Their biggest success was the capture of Vimy Ridge in April 1917 under the command of General Sir Julian Byng. The temptation to name them after the **Bing Boys** – the kings of London theatre-land – was irresistible. After the war, Byng became Governor General of Canada.

C

IS FOR

COLD MEAT TICKET

'C' Company, 5ᵗʰ West Kent Fusiliers,
British Expeditionary Force,
4ᵗʰ July, 1915.

Dear Edward,

I am writing this by candlelight in the <u>Line</u>. The guns have been in action intermittently throughout the day. Just now they are quiet. We are in a <u>billet</u> (well <u>ventilated</u> but with <u>attached roof</u>) which fronts a busy road. The growl of <u>limbers</u>, men and motors outside creates a constant but reassuring hubbub. All the Army's shifting about takes place at night out here, which is one of the reasons we are so tired all the time. <u>Fodder</u> and <u>ammo</u> always get through, but the sleep ration is constantly <u>going short</u> . . . We are being <u>put in</u> for the first time tomorrow, alongside a <u>battalion</u> of <u>Jocks</u>. You can confirm to the kneeses, if they ask, that they do indeed wear their kilts in <u>trenches</u> but under a sort of canvas apron to keep off the filth. This morning they escorted us on a tour of the sector. A lot of them are miners from Fifeshire. I asked one what the <u>Hun</u> was like in these parts and he said, 'He's a gley fly bastarrd, sirr. And he's a dirrty f------ c+-- an' all.' Which sums up the position nicely.

The trenches hereabouts are in a hell of a mess. As fast as the Jocks try to re-build them, the

Hun bashes them in again. Most trench warfare, from what I have seen so far, is _navvying_ under fire. We got a taste of everything on the menu this morning, including heavy stuff and _emma gees._ The worst of it was the death of Sergeant Bremner, our _Company Sergeant Major,_ one of our precious few _regulars._ Our guide was just telling us there was a safe place round the next _traverse,_ when Bremner hopped up for a peek. Instantly, there was a _crack_ like the sound of metal snapping and Bremner's brains spilled like porridge onto his uniform. When he had stopped twitching, Simmonds emptied the poor chap's pockets of _pay book,_ etcetera, and cut away his _cold meat ticket._ The last we saw of him was the soles of his _daisies_ as the _choolie wallahs_ bore him away. The whole Company is in shock. Simmonds is writing to his wife as I write this to you. It is a grim, sad business this game we're playing.

    Yours ever,

    Charles . . .

C of E. Church of England. The abbreviation was stamped on one's **cold meat ticket** to indicate the rites to be observed in the event of death. RC denoted a Roman Catholic, NC a Non Conformist. See also, **'Follow the band'**.

Cack-handed. The correct Army adjective for a clumsy or left-handed person.

Cakehole. The mouth. Army anatomy. See also, **Earhole**.

Cake walk. An easy job. From a promenade dance in America where performers won a cake for producing the most bizarre jazz steps. See also, **Ragtime**.

Camel. A single-seater British fighter biplane made by the Sopwith company. So called because of the humped cowling over its two forward-firing machine guns.

Camouflage. The art of hiding the fact that something is hidden. From the Italian *camuffare*, to disguise.

Canary. A soldier wearing a yellow armband to indicate the specialist nature of his duties, e.g. an instructor at a gas warfare school or a sanitary orderly. More specifically, a canary was a **P.T.** instructor at the **bull ring** at **Eat Apples**.

Candlestick. A bayonet. Although kept sharp for action, most bayonet work in the **infantry**

was domestic. A bayonet stabbed firmly into the wall of a **dug-out** could serve as either candle holder, clothes' hook or both.

Canned Willie, canned horse. American synonyms for **bully**.

Cannon fodder. The **infantry**. From the German *kannone futter*, food for the guns.

Canteen. A place for eating and drinking, usually a hut or marquee. A **wet** canteen sold alcohol, a dry one did not. From the Italian *cantina*, cellar for wine. See **E.F.C.**

Canteen medals. Stains of food or drink on the tunic.

Canuck. A Canadian, originally a French Canadian. The first Canadian regiments got to France three days before Christmas 1914. See also, **Byng Boys**.

Captain. The officer in charge of a **company** in an **infantry battalion**. From the Latin *caput*, head. See also, **Pip**.

Caquot. A French **sausage**. From the name of its inventor. The Caquot could ascend higher than the balloons used by the Germans at the start of the war so when they captured one they copied it and called it a *drachen*, dragon.

'Carry on!' Continue what you are doing! A very common order.

Castor Oil Dragoons. The **R.A.M.C.**, **Royal Army Medical Corps**. From their administration of castor oil in its medicinal form, as a laxative.

Casualty. Any man rendered unavailable for duty. A **battle casualty** was anyone killed, wounded or reported missing. 'It takes 15,000 casualties to train a major general' – Ferdinand Foch.

Casualty Clearing Station, C.C.S. A field hospital attached to a **division**. A C.C.S. had more tents and huts than a **field ambulance** and provided surgery.

Cat meat. A mess of human or animal remains lying in a heap. See also, **Soup**.

Central Powers. The enemy, those nations collectively know as Hunland, i.e. Germany and the Austro-Hungarian Empire, the political entities in the centre of Europe where German was the dominant tongue. They were joined by Turkey in October 1914 and Bulgaria in October 1915. See also, **Ally**.

Chalky. Army nickname for any man called White.

Char. Tea. From the Hindustani *cha*, *chai*, tea. **Sergeant major**'s char was the best – hot, strong and sweet. See also, **Drum up**, **Makings**.

Charger. A strong cavalry horse, capable of bearing a fully equipped cavalryman. Infantrymen applied the word to any horse ridden by an officer. See also, **Hairy**.

Chariot. Any large, powerful car used by **brass**.

Chat. A louse. To chat was to hunt for lice in the seams of one's clothing while conversing with comrades, hence chatting.

Chat bags. Underpants.

Chauffeur. Raymond Poincaré, the French president at the start of the war. His appearance at the **Front** in peaked cap and knickerbockers failed to create a martial impression.

Cheese toaster. A sword or **bayonet**.

Cherry nobs, cherry berries. Military police. See **Red caps**.

Chevron. Correct jargon for the V-shaped **stripes** indicating an N.C.O.'s rank on his sleeve. One stripe – **lance corporal**; two stripes – **corporal**; three stripes – **sergeant**; three stripes and a crown – **sergeant major**. See also, **Lance jack**, **Major**, **Pip**.

Chin parade. An inspection to check men had shaved properly.

China. A chum, a mate. From rhyming slang, china plate.

Chinny, chinni. Sugar. From the Hindustani *chini*.

Chinstrap. In the cavalry the helmet was worn on the point of the chin, **gunners** wore it against their throat. Sometimes, the strap of a **tin lid** was worn backwards, hanging on the nape of the neck, because of a fear that, if it was hit by a shell splinter, it could jerk so violently as to garrotte its wearer. See also, **'Lean on your chinstraps, lads!'**

Chippy. A carpenter. Also, the nickname of any man called Carpenter.

Chit (1), chitty. An Army form, message or suchlike official slip of paper. From the Hindustani *chitthi*, hand-written authorisation. Anyone approaching the **Q.M.** for rations or kit was unlikely to be successful without a chit.

Chit (2). A young female. From Anglo Saxon *kit*, young animal.

Chloride of lime. A white powder disinfectant. It provided the most practicable way of keeping **latrines** tolerable. Chloride of lime was also sprinkled on dead comrades who couldn't be buried properly. See also, **Thunderbox**.

Chlorine. A poisonous gas, first used in battle by **Jerry** at **Eeps**, 22 April 1915. When chlorine came into contact with the lungs it turned into acid.

Choker. Cigarette.

Chuck a dummy. To faint on **parade** with a view to **malingering**.

Chuck it up. To surrender, to do *kamerad*.

Chuck one up. To salute. It was a cornerstone of military discipline that a salute recognised a man's rank not his perceived qualities.

Chum. The most widely used Army synonym for friend. See also, **China**.

Chum, long-eared. A mule.

Chum, long-faced. A horse.

Chum, long-haired. A woman.

Church parade. Compulsory attendance at Sunday service.

C-in-C. Commander-in-Chief. The first C-in-C of the **B.E.F.**, until his mistakes at Loos in 1915, was Sir John French. Thereafter, it was Sir Douglas Haig.

Cipher, cypher. A secret code. From the Arabic *sifr*, empty. The cipher **wallah** was the officer at **I-Branch** charged with devising codes for British **signals** while trying at the same time to decipher **Jerry**'s.

Civvies. Civilian clothes, same as **mufti**.

Civvy. A civilian.

Civvy kip. A bed with a mattress in a bedroom with a roof on it. A rare delight.

Civvy Street. The civilian's place of abode, i.e. **Blighty**.

Clap. Venereal disease. Catching it was considered a form of **malingering** and punished as a **crime**. See also, **Client for Rouen, Phyllis**.

'Clean, bright and slightly oiled.' Literally, the state in which a well-maintained **hipe** was meant to be kept. Colloquially, a hint that someone was inebriated.

Click. To click with a woman was to make her acquaintance without formal introduction. To be clicked by a superior was to be imposed upon for extra duty.

Client for Rouen. A soldier with venereal disease. The **base** at Rouen included several specialist military hospitals. See also, **Red Lamp**.

Clobber. Kit, especially uniform and clothing. From the **Yiddish**.

Clock. The face. Army anatomy. Also, as a verb, to notice something.

C.O. Commanding Officer. C.O. was such a common abbreviation, it became almost a nickname. See also, **O.C., Old Man**.

Coalheavers, Coalies. The Grenadier Guards. In the eighteenth century, officers of this elite regiment quartered at St James's Palace were allowed to hire out their men for common labour; delivering coal was one such sideline.

Cold feet. A symptom of fear, perhaps indicative of having the **wind** up. Any soldier so afflicted might be called a cold footer. Rum in tea was the best-known palliative. Among the French, *avoir mis son pantalon de tremble*, to fill one's trousers.

Cold meat ticket. Soldiers were meant to wear two **identity discs**. In the event of death, one was to be sent home with the personal effects, the other was to remain attached to identify the corpse for burial.

'Come on, tally plonk?' How are you? **Tommy**'s French. From *Comment allez-vous?*

Come the acid. To swagger, to disparage with sarcasm.

Come the double. To take twice as much as one's share.

Come the old soldier. To impose the dignity of one's seniority.

Come it. To attempt any or all of the above. Hence, 'Don't come it with me, son.'

Commission. The document signed by the monarch by which an officer was appointed. As soon as it became clear how many thousands of commissions were going to be needed, the King, George V, stopped signing them personally. A commission can only be taken away by the sovereign, officers therefore keep rank after retiring. From the Latin *commitere*, to entrust. See also, **Temporary gentleman**.

Company. One fourth of an **infantry battalion**. Before the war, a company at full strength was 240 men. During the war it was always much less. See also, **Platoon**.

Conchie. A conscientious objector, one refusing to be a **conscript**. From those who, in the nineteenth century, objected to medical inoculation. See also, **Quaker**.

Concrete macaroon. A **canteen** cake or biscuit.

Concussion. The sudden, violent increase in air pressure caused by an explosion. The bigger the explosion the more damaging the shock wave.

Conk. Nose. Same as **beak** and **boko**.

Conk out. To break down, especially of motor transport.

Conners. Constipation, a consequence of subsisting for weeks on **bully** and **dogs**.

Conscript. A man forced into the Army by the Military Service Act of 27 January 1916, which declared all unmarried male citizens between the ages of 18 and 41 were to be **enlisted**. Compulsory enlistment for married men followed on 25 May 1916. A system of tribunals was set up to hear the arguments of those who felt unable to serve by virtue of ill health, occupation or conscience. See also, **Conchie**, **Derby man**.

Consolidation. Literally, the act of turning captured **Jerry trenches** into British ones by reversing their features, such as **parapets**. Colloquially, consolidation was also applied to making progress with a **bint**.

Cop one. To be wounded, to cop a **packet**.

Cordite. An explosive that came in grey, string-like bundles. See **Ballistite**, **Malingerer**.

CIS FOR COLD MEAT TICKET

Corned dog. See **Bully beef**.

Corp, A **Corporal**, a junior **N.C.O.** Corp was often used as his nickname. From the Latin *corpus*, body. See also, **Chevron**.

'Couldn't hit a cow's arse with a banjo!' The verdict on a poor shot.

Counter battery fire. Artillery firing against artillery. Almost half the shells fired during the war were supposed to have been used against enemy guns.

Countersign. The correct term for the password demanded by **sentries**.

Court martial. A military court. The district court martial and the regimental court martial settled minor crimes. The general court martial and the field general court martial tried the most serious charges such as mutiny and murder. A total of 3,080 men were sentenced to death during the war, of whom some 346 were executed, mostly for desertion.

WILLS'S CIGARETTES.

A TRIBUTE TO THE INFANTRY.

Covering fire. Sustained fire to force the enemy to keep his head down in order to allow one's own change of position or to permit reinforcements to be brought up. Those providing covering fire were known as the covering party.

Cox's, Cox & Co. The London bank patronised by Army

officers. Thousands of **temporary gentlemen** opened an account with Cox & Co. after receiving their **commissions**.

Coy. The written Army abbreviation for an **infantry company**; not Co.

Crabs. Lice. See also, **Chat**.

Crappo. A French trench mortar. From the French *crapaud*, toad.

Crater. A hole caused by the explosion of an underground mine or heavy shell. The biggest crater on the **Western Front** was blown out at La Boiselle, 1 July 1916. It was measured at 100 yards across and 30 yards deep.

Creeping barrage. See **Barrage**.

Cricket ball. A hand grenade introduced in 1915 in time for the Battle of Loos. It was the same shape as a cricket ball but heavier. Widely mistrusted because of its unreliable fuse and the fact that many of them turned out to be **dud**.

Crime. An offence under military law. To crime someone meant to put him on a charge. Any **Tommy** thus charged would have to answer to an officer, who could punish miscreants by stopping pay, removing privileges or imposing **fatigues**. More serious crimes, such as striking a superior or refusing to obey an order, were dealt with by the **Old Man**. A record was kept of a soldier's misdemeanours on Army form 256, his crime sheet. See also, **Court martial**.

Crown and Anchor. An illicit gambling game. It was played with three dice on a cloth (or board) marked out in squares. Each dice was marked with the four suits of cards plus two extra symbols, the crown and the anchor. The heart was known as the puff and dart; the diamond was Kimberley (after the diamond fields of South Africa); the club was the shamrock; the spade was the grave-digger; the anchor was a mud hook; the crown a **sergeant major** or **major** (from his badge of rank). 'Roll up, roll up and put your money down. You've got to speculate to accumulate so who's for the mud hook,

the mucky old anchor? Come on, you lucky lads, if it's the crown you
want, it's the crown you'll back . . .' Players put their stakes on the
squares. The banker, the holder of the 'board', matched each stake
and rolled the dice. Meanwhile, everyone kept look-out for the **red
caps**.

Crucifix corner. It was a French rural custom to mark a crossroads
with a calvary, a figure of the crucified Christ. Several such calvaries
survived bombardment to be incorporated in **trench** lines. The fact
of their survival in the trench lines was taken to be proof of God's
existence. See also, **Joss**.

Crumby. Lousy, crawling with vermin. See also, **Chat**.

Crumpet. The collective noun for attractive women. See also, **Bint**,
Click, **Minge**.

Cup and a wad. Tea and a bun, same as **wet and a wad**.

Cushy. Comfortable, safe, pleasant. From the Hindustani *khush*,
pleasure.

IS FOR

DRUM
UP

'C' Company, 5th West Kent Fusiliers,
British Expeditionary Force,
9th July, 1915.

Dear Edward,

The minstrel boy to the war is gone, the <u>Front
line's</u> where you'll find him. Thankfully, the
trenches have not been too badly knocked about
since the last time we were in and for a change
the <u>neighbours</u> are keeping fairly quiet, perhaps
in the hope that we'll keep quiet too while they
put in a <u>relief.</u> There is almost a hush over the
lines tonight, apart from the occasional rocket
flare shooting up into the dark. My new <u>dug-
out</u> is next but one to <u>Company HQ.</u> There is a
game of cards going on in there, which can only
mean Simmonds has gone out on his rounds
and is not expected back imminently. One of the
<u>corporals,</u> the fatherly Boone, has been prevailed
upon to instruct one of our new lads in his trench
catechism. Mostly, <u>Tommy</u> mistrusts <u>God botherers</u>
and puts no faith in <u>knee drill.</u> The fatalism of
the gambler prevails out here. If a <u>packet</u> has
your <u>name</u> on it you are done for. Corporal Boone
learned the same creed when he was a <u>rookie,</u> from
his corporal's deck of cards, who learned it as a
rookie from his corporal, who learned it as a rookie

from his corporal, back into the mists of time. The Ace in the deck, my lad, refers to the glory of the one true God who reigns over all, indivisible and omnipotent, which means all-powerful so shut up and don't interrupt. The Two in any suit represents His Word, the Old Testament and the New. The Three represents the Father, Son and Holy Ghost. The four stands for the Apostles, Matthew, Mark, Luke and John. The Five is for the five virgins; there were ten, but only five were glorified. The Six stands for the six days it took to create the Heavens and the Earth. The Seven, of course, is for the day God rested. Eight symbolises the family of Noah and his wife, their three sons and their wives, whom God saved from the flood. The Nine are the lepers cleansed by Jesus; he cured ten but nine didn't thank him. The Ten are the ten commandments handed down to Moses on tablets of stone. The Jack reminds us of Satan, one of God's first angels, who was expelled from heaven for his wickedness; he became the Joker of eternal hell and is a warning to us all. The Queen is the Virgin Mary and her son is the King, Jesus Christ, king of kings, born in a stable but raised in glory. When counted, the dots on all the cards add up to 365, that's one for every day of the year. Likewise, the 52 cards in the deck each stand for the 52 weeks in a year. The four suits represent the seasons, spring, summer, autumn and winter. Almanac

and Bible both, that's the soldier's deck of cards,
my lad, and if you learn it well it will guide
you true . . .

    Now then. Whose turn is it to drum up?
Any one of you soppy sods got the makings handy?
Boone's a good man, Edward. Very Greek. We are
all becoming philosophers out here, pitting our
chances against the Fates. Slowly, some element
of the Stoic seems to be taking hold. It's doing a lot
for my education, as you can see.

    Love to all,

    Charles

Dabster, dab hand. Someone trained in a particular military skill, e.g. a **sniper** or **signaller**. A dabster's badge was his recognised insignia.

Daisies. Boots. From rhyming slang, daisy roots. See also, **Ammo**.

Daylight. To put daylight through someone was to pierce him with bullet or blade.

D.C.M., Distinguished Conduct Medal. A **gallantry** award for **Other Ranks**. It dated from 1854 and it was more respected than the new-fangled **Military Medal** of 1916 because any solider who won the D.C.M. got an extra sixpence a day on his pension, if he lived that long.

Dead man's penny. A bronze plaque sent to the relatives of every man who died in uniform. It came with a scroll bearing the King's signature.

Dead soldier. An empty beer bottle, one drained of its life force.

Deader. A dead person, also his funeral.

'Dear Mother, I am sending you ten shillings – but not this week.' One of many chants heard during a march or **fatigue**. Call-and-response chants characterised the humour of the **Other Ranks**. The call, 'Dear Mother, it's a **bugger**! Sell the pig and buy me out!' would be met with the response, 'Dear Son, pig dead, soldier on!'

Debag. To remove someone's trousers by force, perhaps at a **beano**.

Defaulter. A man under punishment for a **crime**. A bugle summoned defaulters to extra **drill** and **fatigues**, a procedure known as doing jankers. See also **Jankers men**.

De-lousing station. A hut or improvised bath house or laundry. **Chats** were supposedly killed by steam and intense heat. After the men had washed they were given disinfected **chat bags** and

greybacks but within hours they would be as **crumby** as ever.

Depot. A **regimental** headquarters in **Blighty** or a **base** for stores in France. From the French *dépôt*, place of deposit.

Derby man. A soldier who **enlisted** in the Army under a scheme devised by the politician Lord Derby. It was introduced in 1915 in a vain effort to postpone the need for **conscription**. A Derby man joined up for a nominal one day and was then sent back to his civilian employment until the Army thought it needed him. Single men were meant to be called up before husbands and fathers.

WILLS'S CIGARETTES.

LATE F.-M. EARL KITCHENER.

Dersie, derzy. The regimental tailor. From the Hindustani *darzi*. He sewed on badges and **gong** ribbons, stitched **stripes** to sleeves and put **pips** on cuffs and shoulders. See also, **Snip**.

Deserter. The military word for any soldier absent from duty without proper reason. To desert was a **crime** punishable by death. See also, **A.W.O.L.**

'Destroyed by shellfire.' A permitted excuse to explain the loss of equipment in **trenches**. If a man judged his load to be too heavy or too dangerous to carry further, it might end up in a shell hole when no one was looking – destroyed by shellfire, no questions asked.

Detachment. The correct jargon for a squad of men or a gun crew.

Deutscher, Dutch. A speaker of *Deutsche*, the German language. See also, **Belgie**.

Devil dodger. A military chaplain. See also, **God botherer**, **Padre**, **Sky pilot**.

Dhoolie wagon. An ambulance.

Dhoolie wallah. Stretcher bearer. From Hindustani, *dhooli*, a litter.

Died of wounds, D.O.W. A **casualty** who died under medical attention. Colloquially, a disparagement of a poor main course at dinner.

Dig in. Troops dug in either when they had reached their objective, to prepare it against counter-attack, or when their attack had failed, as a matter of survival. Colloquially, to dig in was to insinuate oneself with a superior or consolidate one's position with a **bint**.

Digger. An Australian or a New Zealander, an **ANZAC**. From the prospectors who worked the gold fields of Australia. Hence 'up the digger' for 'in the **trenches**'.

Dingo. Mad. Tommy's French. From *dingot*, mad, eccentric.

Dinky. A mule. See **Donk**.

'Dirty that stripe!' An expression from a senior **N.C.O.** on seeing a promoted comrade's new **stripe**. Fresh white **chevrons** were painfully obvious on a grubby, trench-stained tunic sleeve. See also, **Dersie**.

Disinsecting. The process of de-lousing. From the 'Foden Disinfector' machine used in Army laundries. See also, **De-lousing station**.

Ditch. The English Channel. As a verb, to ditch something was to get rid of it. See also, **Drink**.

Ditched. Abandoned, wrecked, out of action. See also, *Kaput*, **Napoo**.

Division. The largest **infantry** formation in an army, commanded by a major-general. Each division consisted of three **brigades** of infantry, plus its own railway train, **Casualty Clearing Station** and **artillery**. Divisions were the chess pieces with which the rival commanders fought their battles.

Divisional Concert Party. See **Follies**, **Gaff**.

Divisional toy shop. The correct sarcasm for a large dump of stores and equipment.

Dixie. A large, oval-shaped bucket for cooking. It had a lid and a handle. From the Hindustani *degchi*, cooking pot.

Dixie bashing. Washing dirty **dixies**, a cookhouse **fatigue**.

'Do you want jam on it as well?' A sarcastic reproof to anyone asking too much, also used to label someone as dissatisfied or ungrateful.

Dock. Hospital, a **Casualty Clearing Station**. Also, the correct military term for a horse's anus. As a verb, to dock someone was to curtail his allowance of pay or rations, either as a punishment or to make up for shortages elsewhere.

Doctor. Nickname for the **Number Nine pill**, given out by the **M.O.** at **sick parade**.

Dodge the column. To deceitfully avoid one's duty, to **malinger**. In German, a column dodger was an *aalemann*, eel-man, a slippery customer, or a *flankenheinrich*, a flank Henry, one clinging to the sidelines. See also, **Swing the lead**.

Dog. Abbreviation of dog biscuit, the ration staple, synonym for **hard tack**.

Dog and maggot. Cheese and biscuit.

Dog with two dicks. To behave like a dog with two dicks was to be gloatingly pleased with one's circumstances to the intense irritation of one's less fortunate comrades. Most commonly applied to one receiving promotion, a generous parcel or notice of **leaf**.

Donk, donkey. A mule, the offspring of a horse and a donkey. See, **Pack animal**.

Donkey walloper. A cavalryman. Also, among **gunners**, a specific disparagement of anyone in the upper-caste **Royal Horse Artillery**.

'Don't tear the arse out of it!' Gently! Take it easy!

Dooly, doolay. Milk. *Tommy*'s French. From *du lait*, milk.

Dora, D.O.R.A. The Defence of the Realm Act. It was passed in five minutes, 8 August 1914, and gave the government powers to introduce any measure deemed necessary to defend the nation, including censorship, imprisonment without trial and suchlike infringements of traditional British liberties. One of Dora's impositions that lingered on after the war was the introduction of daylight saving hours, putting the clocks forward and back in summer and winter.

Doughboy. An American soldier, a **Yank**. The United States entered the war in April 1917 but the American Expeditionary Force, **A.E.F.**, didn't see combat on the Western Front until 1918. When the Yanks arrived some British newspapers tried to give them the nickname Sammies, after the figure of **Uncle Sam**, but it didn't catch on.

D.O.W. See **Died of wounds**.

Downwind. To be downwind was to be in a bad-smelling place or a **hot spot**.

D-phone. An early type of **buzzer** for sending messages in **Morse code** along a copper wire. See also, **Buzz**.

Draw stumps. To end a job of work or break off from a fight. From cricket. The opposite of to **open the bowling**.

Dreadnought. Literally, a powerful, well-armoured battleship. Colloquially, a rubber prophylactic for use in the event of **clicking** with a mam'selle. See also, **French letter**.

Drill. To be ordered through a sequence of military movements until they could be repeated flawlessly without thinking. The preferred Army method of instruction. Each task was broken down into functions which could be learned as a sequence. 'What's the drill here?' was therefore the proper question from a soldier encountering anything new or unfamiliar.

Drink. The English Channel. See also, **Ditch**.

Driver's pint. A gallon. Driving horse teams was thirsty work.

'Dropped out of my hands.' A routine excuse for a breakage.

Drop Shots, Drop Shorts. Derogatory nicknames for any **gunners** known or suspected to have hit their own **infantry**.

Drum. The circular, plate-sized pan of ammunition for the **Lewis gun**, a machine gun. From its resemblance to a drumhead. There were two sizes of drum, one held 48 **rounds**, the other 97. See also, **Pannier**.

Drum up. To collect men together, to muster the troops. Also, to **brew** tea. As in, 'Go and **scrounge** some **dooly** and we'll drum up.'

Duckboard. Slatted frames of wood for flooring muddy **trenches**. Duckboards could be slotted into a wooden frame or laid flat on the trench floor. Duckboard was also a mildly disparaging way of referring to the ribbon of the **Military Medal**, which consisted of several multi-coloured bars.

Dud. A failure, any weapon or device that did not work. Specifically, **bombs** or shells that did not explode. Dud also applied to people. Reinforcements arriving at a **battalion** in the **Line** were quickly assessed for the duds among them.

WILLS'S CIGARETTES.

A TRIBUTE TO THE ROYAL ARTILLERY

Dug-out. An underground **trench** shelter. Its entrance always faced away from enemy shellfire. It was reckoned that the roof of a dug-out needed to be 15 feet below the surface to be **shell** proof. The French word was *abri*, shelter.

Dumb insolence. To greet an order with an expression of incredulity or contempt. A military **crime**. Farting on **parade** came under the same heading. See also, **Lip**.

Dung hampers. Riding breeches, as worn by **donkey wallopers** and **gunners**.

Duration. Abbreviation of the phrase 'duration of the war'. Men who joined up in 1914–15 volunteered for 'three years or the duration of the war'. Such a volunteer was sometimes known as a duration man. Hence the yearning exclamation, uttered in moments of weariness or stress, 'Roll on duration', **R.O.D.**

IS FOR

ESTAMINY

'C' Company, 5th West Kent Fusiliers,
British Expeditionary Force,
7th July, 1915.

Dear Mudge,

I am back in the <u>billets</u> I told you about for a bit
of a <u>rest</u>. I have just gorged on a feast of mail
and am sipping a nice café au lait in the local
<u>estaminy</u>. Forget the French word 'estaminet', this
is <u>Tommy's</u> version, a cross between a café, public
house, concert room and grocery. The menu is
unambitious, omelettes or similar. The wine
list is terse, <u>red ink or plonk.</u> The bill of fare
is not the point. Nothing bucks your fighting man
more than to carouse with his mates in a warm
fug of tobacco smoke, attended by women. In our
<u>trenches</u> and <u>dug-outs</u> we are part of the war. In
the estaminy we are restored.

Which brings me, dearest M, to my urgent
request. <u>Fags!</u> You will understand how important
they are when I say they represent almost the
only pleasure the Army does not regard as a
<u>crime.</u> In recognition of this it supplies tobacco
as <u>issue.</u> However, as you can imagine, the lads
take a pretty poor view of what the <u>Quarter-bloke</u>
dishes out as an acceptable smoke. Here's what
I would like you to do. Buy me two of the biggest
tins possible of <u>Abdullas</u> and Gold Flake. Then

procure a commodious cigarette case, one with two compartments, like the one Simmonds got from Asprey's I think. I can then fill one half with fags for fellow officers and the other with fags for the men, depending on the circs. Make sure you disguise the parcel well. Wrap the tins around with coggidge to make them look lumpy and uninteresting. Send the fag case separately, perhaps in a hollowed-out book. It is surprising how easily desirable and expensive perquisites quite often go missing on their journey up the line. I am enclosing a cheque which should cover the fags and my immediate demands. I am also thinking of buying a gramaphone. Could I trouble you to send me a catalogue? No rush. Give Fudge my filial regards. Tell him that, as ever, I remain in the pinkest of condition and that I never stop thinking of home and what you might all be doing.

Best love,

Charlie

Earhole. To approach someone about borrowing something. 'I earholed him for a **fag** but he said he was all out, the **bloody** liar.'

Earwiggers. Headphones, for buzzer work. From the official Army verb, earwig, to eavesdrop, to pay close attention to what's being said. See also, **Buzz**.

Easterner. A politician or general who argued that Germany could be weakened to the point of collapse by attacks in the East, i.e. through the Balkans, Turkey and the Black Sea. The strategic opponent of a **Westerner**. See also, **Flank**.

Eat Apples, Eatables. Tommy's French for Etaples, on the French coast, near the port of Boulogne. The British **base** there eventually covered five square miles.

Eeps. The Belgian town of Ypres. See **Salient**.

E.F.C. Expeditionary Force **Canteen**. See also, **Valroy water**.

Effective strength. The number of men in a unit available for duty, i.e. excluding the detached, the sick, those on **leaf** or those attending some course of instruction.

Egg. A hand grenade or bomb. An actual egg bomb was the size of a hen's egg. It could be thrown further than a **Mills bomb** but did less damage. See also, **Pill**.

Egyptian medal. A fly button on a pair of trousers. 'I see you're wearing your Egyptian medal today' was a warning to a comrade that his flies were undone, thereby committing the military **crime** of being improperly dressed.

'Eh!?' This interrogatory exclamation was strictly discouraged as a reply to any **N.C.O.**'s question, order or remark. '"Eh!?"' would be the response. 'Are you saying "eh" to me, lad? You'll be saying "arseholes" to the colonel next!' See also, **Dumb insolence**, **Lip**.

Eight, one over the. One drink too many. A gallon of beer (eight pints) was the measure of an adequate night's consumption. See also, **Driver's pint**.

Emergency ration. Official term for the **iron ration**: a tin of **bully**; a packet of tea; sugar; **dog** biscuits. No man was allowed to eat his iron ration without an order. The phrase also was applied to **regimental mascots**.

Emma gee. Machine gun. From the initials M. and G. in **Signalese**.

Enfilade fire. To fire obliquely at the enemy rather than from in front of or behind him. Military jargon. Enfilade fire was particularly effective if it could be brought to bear from opposite sides at the same time. Two streams of enfilade fire could create an impenetrable storm of bullets. It was to prevent the enfilade of **trenches** that they were dug with **traverses**. From the French *enfiler*, to string beads on a thread.

Enlist. The correct verb for the act of joining the Army as a **private**. Officers did not enlist, they received the King's **commission**.

Erfs. Eggs. **Tommy**'s French. From *oeufs*, eggs. Also, deserfs from *des oeufs*, some eggs. Also, doozerfs from *deux oeufs*, two eggs. *Oeufs* could also be pronounced oofs.

Estaminy. A makeshift café-bar serving the basic amenities for men in **billets**.

Evaporation. The scientific explanation for the disappearance of any precious liquid, such as rum, during its transit from the **base** to the **Front**. See also, **S.R.D.**

Exasperator. A respirator gas mask. Awkward to fit, awkward to wear.

IS FOR

FORNICATION

'C' Company, 5th West Kent Fusiliers,
British Expeditionary Force,
6th August, 1915.

Dear Edward,

The latest gup, straight from the Colonel's horse,
is that we have been given a proper job to do, which
will make a change from squatting in these filthy
trenches being stonked by the supercilious Hun
whenever he feels like it. It also involves a change
of locale, for which we are most grateful. These
particular lodgings were much fought over before
we came in and, what with the continuous warm
weather, the stench of mortality from the glorious
dead can be quite offensive if you trip over one
on patrol. On the way back from our recce of the
new trenches we popped in to our nearest intact
town to stock up on necessaries for the mess. As
we wandered along, enjoying the sheer luxury of
being in a proper street again, we took a turn
down a rue with a Red Lamp in it. That's a brothel
to you, young fellow, or what the French military
authorities call a maison tolerée. Red Lamps are
for the Other Ranks, Blue Lamps are for officers,
although whether this is because of a difference in
the quality of the merchandise I cannot be sure.
At the Base, of course, Tommy need never go
short of hired companionship but I was surprised

to find the second-oldest profession so well dug-in
so far up the Line. While we were standing there,
somewhat agape at the motley of ranks queuing
down the street, a couple of red tabs arrived to meet
their chariot. They spotted a couple of Indians
in the crowd. 'Keen on their fornication, ain't
they?' observed one to the other. 'Oh yes,' came
the reply (he was presumably an old India hand).
'They're keen on white rabbit if they can get hold
of it.' I was entranced, as you can imagine –
white rabbit!?? 'Let's hope,' murmured the first,
'they're as keen on their fighting, when the time
comes.' How can anyone at home doubt that we will
prevail?

Tails up!

Your Charles

Fag. A cigarette.

Fairy lights. Sarcasm for the effect of distant explosions at night, specifically of coloured signal rockets. See also, **Fireworks**.

'Fall in!' The order to form a line to await further orders. It was often given out by **N.C.O.**s as 'Get fell in!' Once fallen in, men were on **parade**.

Fall out. To collapse in a heap at the side of the road while marching. A **crime**.

Fang. Army vernacular for tooth.

Fang farrier. Army dentist. Part of a proper farrier's job was to extract worn nails from horses' hooves in order to re-shoe them.

Fanny. A female volunteer in the First Aid Nursing Yeomanry, F.A.N.Y., which ran ambulances and staffed hospitals. See also, **Minge**.

Fart sack. Sleeping bag. Part of an officer's kit. See also, **Flea bag**, **Valise**.

Farting Fanny. British nickname for a German heavy gun used to bombard the French city of Arras between 1915–16.

Fatten up. The process of training troops for a particular **stunt**. They would be taken behind the **Line** and **drilled** intensively while being well fed and looked after. See also, *Frontschwein*.

Fatigue. A routine military chore of a domestic nature. Digging **trenches**, **humping** stores and emptying **latrine** buckets were typical fatigues. Men in a fatigue party were usually supervised by a **lance jack**. Extra fatigues were imposed as punishment for minor offences. The word was sometimes pronounced fatti-gew.

Feldgrau. The **Jerry** word for field-grey, the colour of his uniform. Grey was sometimes used by the British to refer to German infantry in the mass. To **fire into the grey** was to fire into the mass rather than to choose an individual Jerry as one's target.

Fernleaves. New Zealanders. From their national badge, a fern leaf. See **ANZAC**.

Field ambulance. A field ambulance was not a vehicle, it was a military hospital of tents and huts with a staff of some 200 officers and men, including **stretcher bearers**, nurses, cooks, etc. From the French *ambulant*. See also, **Fanny**, **V.A.D.**

Field cashier. An army paymaster, the Buckshee King. Company officers collected pay from the field cashier and gave it out at pay parade, entering the amount in each soldier's **pay book**. A shilling a day was the basic pay of an **infantry private**, plus any specialist's pay to which he was entitled, less deductions imposed as a punishment. See also, **Buckshee**, **Ring money**.

Field day. A military exercise in which commanders and their **staff** practised battles with real troops fighting an imaginary enemy. **Having a field day** was the phrase used on those occasions when a **show** went according to plan against the real enemy.

Field dressing. The first aid packet sewn inside every infantryman's tunic. It contained two bandages and safety pins.

Field glass. Telescope.

Field glasses. Binoculars.

Field-grey. See *Feldgrau*.

Field postcard. An Army form issued as a postcard, printed with stereotypical phrases to be crossed out if not required. '*I am quite well. I have been admitted into hospital {sick/ wounded} and am going on well/ and hope to be discharged soon. I am being sent down to the base. I have received your {letter dated _____/ telegram dated _____/ parcel dated _____} Letter follows at first opportunity. I have received no letter from you {lately/ for a long* *time}. {Signature only} Date* _____. *[Postage must be prepaid on any letter or postcard addressed to the sender of this card]'* The field postcard was called a quick-firer or **whizz-bang** because it got to **Blighty** quicker than a letter, which was often held up because it had to be censored by an officer.

Field punishment number one. A severe punishment. The offender was lashed to a gun wheel by his ankles and wrists for one hour in the morning and one hour in the evening. The diet was bread and water.

Field Survey. The correct jargon for the Army's mapping service. It started the war as one officer and a clerk at **G.H.Q.** By 1918 it consisted of 400 officers and 6,000 men. Known colloquially as **the Survey**.

Filly. Literally, a female horse fit for breeding. Colloquially, a young woman.

'Fire into the grey!' See *Feldgrau*.

Fire trench. A **trench** organised and equipped for firing at the enemy. A fire trench consisted of **traverses** and fire bays. The fire bay was a straight section of trench facing the enemy, about ten yards in length with room for several riflemen. It had a firestep for standing

WILLS'S CIGARETTES.

MOTOR SEARCHLIGHT.

PASSED FOR PUBLICATION BY THE PRESS BUREAU. 21-9-15?

on, a **parapet** with loopholes for firing through and a **parados** at the back.

Fireworks, firework display. An intense or prolonged artillery bombardment at night, accompanied by **infantry signal** flares coded red, white, yellow and green. See also, **S.O.S.**, **Very light**.

Flag-wagger. A **signaller**. The alphabet for flag signalling was semaphore.

Flak. German slang for **Archie**, an abbreviation of *flugabwehrkanonen*.

Flaming onions. One of **Jerry**'s anti-aircraft weapons, the *lichtspucker*, light spitter. It fired incendiary phosphorous flares in quick succession so that they looked like a string of blazing onions going up into the sky.

Flammenwerfer. A **Jerry** flame-thrower, first encountered at Hooge near **Eeps**, 30 July 1915. It was a terrifying weapon when it first appeared but not very good at killing. If men stayed down in their **trenches**, the stream of flaming oil shot harmlessly over their heads.

Flank. Military jargon for the side of something. To move into a position whereby **Jerry** could be attacked sideways (or from behind) was to outflank him. **Refused flank** was officers' jargon for positioning men at an angle to their **Front**, in order to ward off an enemy flanking manoeuvre. See also, **Easterner**, **Enfilade**.

Flapper. A teenage girl with a saucy demeanour. She wore high heels, short skirts and powdered her face. Flapper was also used of an **Ayrton fan**.

Flapper's delight. A **temporary gentleman** seeking a good time on **leaf**.

Flea bag. Sleeping bag. See also, **Fart sack**, **Valise**.

Flog. To sell. It was a **crime** to flog Army kit or stores to **Belgies** or **Frogs**.

Flop. A failure, a **stunt** or **show** ending in a **lash-up**.

Flying arsehole. An observer in the **Royal Flying Corps**. His badge was the letter 'O' with a wing attached. Observing was not his only function, he also fired his plane's **emma gee**. See also, **Mister Sandbags**.

Flying coffin. Any type of aircraft regarded as hazardous to fly.

Flying corpse. A punning nickname for a pilot, derived from the brevity of his useful span. In 1916 the average life expectancy of a pilot in the **Royal Flying Corps** was three weeks; in 1917 it was six weeks.

Flying matinee. A **trench** raid carried out in daylight.

Flying pig. A heavy bomb from a **trench mortar**.

Fodder. Food. See **Nosebag**.

Follies. Troupes of entertainers raised from within the ranks to provide comic relief to **divisions** at **rest** behind the lines.

'Follow the band.' To do the same as everyone else in matters of religion. 'What's your persuasion, lad?' 'I'll follow the band.' '**C of E** it is, then.' See also, **Joss**.

Football. A type of British **trench mortar** bomb. From its spherical appearance. For firing, the football full of explosive had to be attached to a stalk to fit inside the mortar tube. Once this was done it became a **toffee apple**.

Footslogger. An infantryman. To footslog was to march at 30 inches to the pace; 108 paces to the minute; 50 minutes to the hour followed by 10 minutes' rest. The average speed of British footsloggers carrying their full load was about three miles per hour.

Forage cap. The official Army hat, with a round flat crown and a visor. See also, **Gorblimey**.

'Form squares to receive cavalry!' An old Army order used ironically to warn of the imminent arrival of something (or someone) nasty.

Fornication. The correct Army word for sex. Fighting, drinking and fornicating were held to be the main concerns of the well-adjusted warrior, as evidenced by his **lingo**. See also, **Hump**, **Jiggy-jig**, **Jump**, **Kindness**, **Roger**.

Frahnsay. Tommy's French. From *Français*. The language of **Frogs**.

Fray Bentos. A ubiquitous brand of **bully**, named after the town in Uruguay where it was canned, home of the largest cold store in the world.

French letter. A prophylactic sheath. See also, **Dreadnought**.

Fritz. A **Jerry**, from the diminutive form of Friedrich. Early in the war it was a more common nickname than Jerry. Fritz was also used by the German infantry of themselves. Jerry called his **gunner** comrade Ernst.

Frock. The disparaging military word for a politician, from the frock coat he wore.

Froggie, Frog. A French person. Derived from frogs' legs in garlic, a delicacy of the French table.

Frong. Francs, the French currency. One franc was reckoned to be worth a **tanner**. See also, **Onks**.

Front, the. The **trench** lines and the country on either side within range of their. It was named the **Western Front** by the Germans; they had another one in the East, facing Russia.

Frontschwein. Literally, in German, front-hogs. **Jerry** lived in mud while being readied for the mincing machine, same as **Tommy**. See also, **Fatten up**.

Fruit salad. Two or more rows of medal ribbons worn on the tunic.

Fullerphone. A British device for transmitting **Morse code** along a copper wire. It had two circuits; one carried a continuous **buzz**; the other carried the actual signals in Morse. **Jerry** could only pick up the buzz. Named after its inventor, Captain A. C. Fuller.

Fumigator. A machine to destroy **chats**, found in laundries and hospitals. Fumigation was also the guaranteed way to shrink one's uniform. See also, **Disinsecting**.

Funk. Fear. To be in a funk was to be scared. To be in a blue funk was to be very scared. To be in a raging blue funk was to be very, very scared. See also, **Wind**.

Fusilier. Army jargon for a **private** in a fusilier **regiment**. A private in a rifle regiment was a rifleman. In the sixteenth century, when muskets were fired by a lighted match, the invention of the fusil, which was fired by a flintlock (Italian *fucile*, flint) represented a leap forward in firearms. Fusiliers remained an elite until the introduction of the rifle made light infantry a key force. Hence the rivalry between fusiliers and rifle regiments. Fusilier was a calculated insult from a rifleman when it was pronounced fusi-*liar*.

IS FOR

GONG

'C' Company, 5th West Kent Fusiliers,
British Expeditionary Force,
19th August, 1915.

Dear Fudge,

    Yesterday I slept almost the whole day through
after the most exhilaratingly horrible and
downright interesting experience of my entire life.
You may have guessed, from the tone of recent
letters, that something was about to happen. Well
now it has – our first proper <u>show</u>. Not a battle,
but a necessary part of the work that is going on
to get us into one. We <u>hopped over</u> from Gunner's
Farm Trench, with the <u>Jocks</u> supplying <u>covering
fire</u> from our left. Our specific objective was a
machine gun post in <u>Jerry's</u> line known to us as
'the Nose'. Two <u>platoons</u> of 'A' <u>Coy</u> went over
on the left and two platoons of 'C' Coy on the
right. The <u>guns were to lay on two barrages</u>, one
on Jerry's front line and the other behind it, to
prevent his reinforcements getting <u>up</u>. Captain
Simmonds put me and Sergeant Sullivan in
charge of the first charge. What no one had reckoned
on, unfortunately, was that, to our right, Brother
<u>Bosche</u> had another machine gun so sited as to
<u>enfilade</u> our line of attack. No one knew about this
gun. It had never fired a shot since our arrival
at Gunner's Farm. But as the smoke cleared,

there was <u>Fritz</u> bobbing up and down behind his <u>parapet</u> getting into action with all guns blazing. Sergeant Sullivan seized the man next to him and they threw themselves forward, with me urging the rest of 'C' Coy to follow suit. Sullivan got one man through the throat with his <u>toasting fork</u> then dropped another with a snap shot from the kneeling position. I stood there pooping off my <u>Webley</u> at anything that moved. When it was empty, instead of re-loading I threw it in some ugly Bosche's face. Fortunately, Empson kept his nerve and hurried Jerry on his way with some cool work from the bombers. Captain Simmonds then arrived with the rest of the Coy to start <u>consolidating</u>. We found Sergeant Sullivan slumped against the Nose's machine gun, covered in blood. That evening, after the wounded had been taken down, I made my report and recommended that Sullivan's <u>gallantry</u> be recognised. Today I heard the result. He <u>died of wounds</u> at the <u>C.C.S.</u> Captain Simmonds has been recommended for the <u>Military Cross</u> and the <u>brigadier</u> has approved it. I think we are all to be rewarded with a spell of <u>Rest,</u> so I can write more anon.

Your affectionate son,

Charles

'G', G-branch. The branch of **staff** work concerned with General Duties, i.e. fighting.

Gaff. A concert, as laid on by the **Divisional Concert Party**. Also, a sing-song with perhaps a piano accompaniment from the **padre**. See also, **Blow the gaff**.

Gallantry. The official Army word for bravery in battle. See also, **Gong**.

Galloper. A mounted officer attached to a general's staff for carrying despatches.

Gallops, the. A bad case of diarrhoea or dysentery. See also, **Trots**.

Galloping Lockharts. The field kitchens, large vats for cooking or brewing tea in **battalion**-sized quantities. Guaranteed to make the **burgoo** taste like stew.

Gangrene. The putrefaction of a wound caused by constriction of blood flow. Once gangrene had set in amputation was likely to follow. See also, **Bully gas**.

Garniture. Vegetation on a **camouflage** net. From the French *garnir*, to garnish.

Garrison sports. A thorough spring clean of barracks, camp or **billet**.

Gas alarm. In **trenches**, the usual gas alarm was an empty shell case banged with a stick or **bayonet**. **Jerry** used three main types of gas. Lachrymatory gases made men cry and sent them blind temporarily. Asphyxiants choked men by turning to acid in their lungs. Blistering agents brought the skin out in burns and corroded the eyeballs.

Gas alert. The state of preparedness for a gas attack. When on alert men wore their gas masks on their chests so they could be put on quickly.

Gas bag. The square-ish knapsack in which the gas mask was carried. Also, a **sausage**.

Gas chamber. A sealed hut filled with gas for testing gas masks and for training troops in their use.

Gas curtain. Sacking or a blanket hung over the entrance to a **dug-out** to keep out gas. It had to be soaked with a chemical called **hypo** for maximum effectiveness.

Gas face. A gas mask. The rubber mask covering the face and nose was first introduced by the Germans in 1915 – the *gummimaske*. In the British version, a tube connected the mask to a box-like filter of chemicals, hence box **respirator**. Masks had replaced hoods by the beginning of 1917.

Gas gong. See Gas Alarm.

Gas hood. See '**Goggle-eyed bugger with the tit**', P-helmet.

'Gas us.' The request for soda water or carbonated mineral water to be added to a drink. Officers' French. From **gazeuse**, carbonated, fizzy.

Gazette. The British government newspaper, the *London Gazette*. To be gazetted was to have one's name published in the *Gazette*. Military and naval appointments or promotions became official once they had been gazetted, likewise the granting of **gallantry** awards and other honours. See also, **Mentioned in Despatches**.

Gentleman's relish. A potted savoury paste for spreading on **hard tack** to make it palatable to officers. Welcome in any food parcel.

Geophone. A device like a stethoscope used by tunnellers to detect vibration underground, thereby providing warning of enemy counter-mining. See **Sapper**.

German sausage. A **Jerry** observation balloon. See, *Caquot*, **Sausage**.

'Get busy, lads!' A phrase often used by **N.C.O.**s when handing out **micks (2)** and **banjos**.

Get down to it. Blessed sleep. In **trenches**, men existed in a perpetual state of near exhaustion from lack of **kip**. On reaching **billets** after coming out of the **Line** it was not uncommon for them to sleep where they fell.

Get in the way of. To be hit. 'Poor **bugger**, he got in the way of a **whizz-bang**.'

'Get your ears put back!' An **N.C.O.**'s phrase for ordering a man to get his hair cut, i.e. to make his ears wholly visible again. See also, **'Am I hurting you?'**

G.H.Q., General Headquarters. The first **C-in-C**, Commander-in-Chief of the **B.E.F.**, Sir John French, established his G.H.Q. at St Omer. His successor, Sir Douglas Haig, moved it to Montreuil, which was closer to the Channel port of Boulogne and **Eat Apples**.

Ginger. Any man called Jones, whether he had red hair or not.

Ginger up. To energise, to rouse to a higher pitch of enthusiasm. See also, **Jildy**.

'Give your arse a chance!' An injunction to a comrade to stop talking rubbish. As in, 'Shut your **cakehole** and . . .'

Glory hole. A small-ish **dug-out**.

Go crook. To report sick. Australian derivation.

Go over. To go over the top meant to leave one's **trench** the front way, over the **parapet**, for an expedition into **No Man's Land**. See also, **Hop over**, **Zero**.

Go short. To be deprived of something, perhaps as a punishment, perhaps because of incompetence down the **Line**.

Go up. To proceed from the **base** to the **Front**, to go **up** the **Line**. Also, to explode, as in, 'A shell hit the dump and it went up like bonfire night.'

Go west. To be killed. One derivation invokes the setting sun, going down in the west. Another suggests an origin in the execution of criminals at Tyburn, near Marble Arch in London, on the road west from the city, where convicts were hanged. Compare the French *être évacué sur une toile de tente*, to be despatched in a canvas sheet, *avoir la grande permission*, to get a long spell of leave, or *gagner la croix de bois*, to win the Order of the **Wooden Cross**.

God botherer. Padre, chaplain. See also, **Devil dodger**, **Sky pilot**.

God squad. Christian soldiers.

God's Own. A nickname applied sarcastically to any unit deemed to think too highly of its accomplishments. See also, **Nobody's Own**.

'Goggle-eyed bugger with the tit.' The phrase for a man wearing a **gas hood**. It had fitted **goggles** and a rubber teat in the middle for breathing through the mouth.

Goggles. Spectacles. From which goggle-eyed to describe a spectacle wearer.

Going. The state of the terrain. **Footsloggers** launching an attack always wanted to know if the going might help or hinder. From the racecourse, where the going was rated heavy, soft, good to soft, good, good to firm, firm.

Goldfish. Tinned salmon or sardines.

Gold stripe. A strip of braid worn above the cuff of the left sleeve to indicate each time the wearer had been wounded. Introduced in 1916. **Thrusters** derided such adornment. 'You're in the Army, for God's sake! It's your duty to get wounded!'

Golden Virgin. See **Lady of the Limp**.

Gong. A medal. **Jerry**'s equivalent disparagement was *zinnware*, tin-wear. The French phrase was *batterie de cuisine*, pots and pans. See also, **Putty medal**, **Rooti medal**.

Gong hunter. A soldier keen to win his medal.

'Good-bye-ee!' This attenuated pronunciation of goodbye derived from a music-hall song. '*Bon soir*, old thing! Cheer-i-o! Chin chin! **Napoo!** Toodle-oo! Good-bye-ee!'

Goodnight kiss. The last shot fired by a **sniper** at the end of his day's work.

'Goody-la!' Exclamation deriving from Chinese labour battalions and adopted by those who came into contact with them as a term of approbation.

Goolies. The testicles. From the Hindustani *gooli*, a pellet. See also, **Orchestra**.

Gor Blimey! Gorblimey. Euphemism instead of a swear word. A gorblimey cap was the Army's **forage cap** with its wire stiffener taken out to make it fashionable.

Gorget. The tab of cloth worn on the collar of an officer's tunic. Generals and full colonels in rank wore a scarlet tab. Different colours were worn according to which branch of the **staff** an officer was working in.

Gramaphone. Original name for a record player, from which the music issued via a large horn. A portable gramophone in its carrying case, such as the Decca, was an esteemed amenity in the **dug-outs** of smart young **subalterns**.

Grandma, granny. All-purpose nickname for a **heavy** gun or **how**.

Gravy. Petrol.

Grease. Butter. See **Axle grease**.

Greatcoat. The thick, Army overcoat issued to **Other Ranks**. It fell to below the knees.

Great White Hope. The mythical stratagem or winning weapon that would bring victory. From the search in the United States for a white boxer capable of wresting the world heavyweight title away from the black champion, **Jack Johnson**.

Green one, green envelope. An Army envelope for private correspondence. The user had to swear that the letter inside contained no information of value to the enemy. Ordinarily, letters had to be read and censored by officers. See **Sticky Jack**.

WILLS'S CIGARETTES.

A TRIBUTE TO THE ROYAL FLYING CORPS

Green tab. An Intelligence officer. From the colour of his **gorgets**. See **I-Branch**.

Grenade. A bomb, for throwing. From pomegranate (Latin *pommum*, apple, *grenate*, having many seeds). See also, **Mills bomb**, **Potato masher**.

Greyback. An Army shirt. It was made of grey flannel and had tin buttons. Officers paid for their own **khaki** shirts.

Grog. A mixture of rum and water.

G.S.W., Gun Shot Wound. A medic's abbreviation for labelling a bullet wound.

Guards. The elite of **infantry**, the sovereign's bodyguard. Until the war, there were four **regiments**: Grenadier Guards; Coldstream Guards; Scots Guards; Irish Guards. The Welsh Guards were formed in 1915, the year all Guards **battalions** were brought together to form the Guards **Division**. See also, **Coalheavers**.

Guardsman. The correct term for a **private** in the **Guards**. He buttoned his tunic according to the **regiment** he was in. The Grenadiers wore their buttons evenly spaced; the Coldstream in pairs; the Scots Guards in threes; the Irish Guards in fours; the Welsh Guards in fives.

Gun. Strictly speaking, a gun was an **artillery piece** with an elevation of less than 20 degrees from the horizontal. The barrel of a **howitzer** could be raised as high as 45 degrees. The word piece covered both types of weapon. See also, **How**.

Gun fodder. Infantry, food for the **guns**. See also, **Cannon fodder**, **Fatten up**.

Gun layer. The member of a gun crew responsible for aiming it.

Gunfire. The first brew of **char** of the day.

Gunner. An artilleryman, any soldier in any branch of the **artillery**.

Gup. Gossip picked up in a **canteen** or **estaminy**. From the Hindustani *gap*, prattle.

Gut's horn. The bugle call to announce meal times.

IS FOR

HUN

'C' Company, 5th West Kent Fusiliers,
British Expeditionary Force,
25th August, 1915.

Dear Edward,

    I have been in <u>dock</u> for a few days but don't tell
the people. Mudge worries far too much as it is
and in any case I was not hurt badly. Something
grazed the back of my right thigh in last
Wednesday's <u>show</u>, not enough to give me a limp.
I also had my left earlobe torn off. It hardly bled
but when I woke up the next day the whole left side
of my face was numb and exceedingly painful and
the <u>M.O.</u> packed me off to the <u>Casualty Clearing
Station.</u> Close shaves do not come much closer,
which is another reason to keep M & F in the dark.
They will only fret that I am using up my luck,
which is true. One day I will <u>cop one</u> and they can
grieve to their heart's content. Until then they
should be kept in blissful ignorance. I wrote Fudge
a partial account of the fight but left out my
wounds so I am counting on you to keep mum.
You are slightly off course, by the way, to write as
you do of 'blood lust'. There is such an urge and it
was active last week but I personally did not feel
it. What I felt at first was fear and bewilderment
but once I had mastered myself what came through
was an intense exhilaration such as I have only

encountered previously while hunting. I bagged two _Huns_ for certain. My first was on one knee taking aim. I got him with a lucky shot in his ribs and when he keeled over one of our lads got onto him with his bayonet to make sure. The second Hun was down in the _trench_, unpacking _potato mashers_ from a box. He looked up, with a _bomb_ in each hand, and knew he was done for. I _plugged_ him smack in the face and kept firing until my _Webley_ was empty at which point one of his _kamerads_ came scurrying round the _traverse_. I threw my pistol at him and he turned and ran. We have got the licking of them, Eddie. Your average _Jerry_ simply cannot win against an Englishman, even though he is better equipped and trained for this kind of warfare. He is ahead of us in kit, tactics and discipline but we are learning from him all the time and, man for man, when we get him in a tight corner we will always come out on top.

Yours, bloody but unbowed,

Chazzer

H.A.C., Honourable Artillery Company. The oldest recorded **regiment** in the British Army, raised by Henry VIII in 1537. Not an **artillery** unit but a **regiment** of **terriers** recruited mainly from business and professional types in the City of London. Nickname, the Home and Colonial. Members paid a two-guinea yearly subscription, which provoked incredulity on the **Western Front**. 'You mean you've paid to be here?'

'Had it!' Broken, finished. See also, *Kaput*, **Napoo**.

Hair brush. An early type of hand grenade. It consisted of a wooden paddle, the size and shape of a hair brush, with a **box of tricks** attached.

WILLS'S CIGARETTES

Hairy. An Army cart horse. From the long hair on its fetlocks. The 60-pounder gun, weighing more than four tons, was hauled by a team of ten.

Hairy arsed. All-purpose insult, useful for inflaming regimental rivalries in an **estaminy**.

Half-crown brigade. Generic nickname for any **mob** identified by the designation 2nd/6th, e.g. 2nd/6th West Kent Fusiliers. From the silver half-crown which was worth two shillings and sixpence, written 2s/6d.

Half-inch. To pinch, steal. From rhyming slang. To be cheated was to be half-ounced.

Half-right. To the right, at an angle of about 45 degrees. Likewise, half-left. Approximate Army measurements. See also, **Armful**.

Ham bags. Female underwear.

Hand Cart Cavalry. Stokes mortar units. From the miniature wagons they used for transporting their gear. Wilfred Stokes worked at the Ipswich engineering firm Ransomes. The **trench mortar** he invented was cheap and light – a length of tubing with collapsible legs that could be carried comfortably on a man's shoulder. The Stokes could fire 20–30 bombs per minute and had a range of nearly half a mile when it was first introduced in 1916. Several Stokes bombs could be in the air simultaneously and could destroy a **Jerry** post within seconds.

Hard tack. The Army ration biscuit. Soft tack was bread. In addition to its nutritional function, hard tack was sometimes used as kindling for fires. See also, **Dog**.

Hard tail. A mule. See **Donk**.

Harker. A member of a listening patrol sent into **No Man's Land** to detect enemy movements. Harker was also the nickname for any device designed to improve eavesdropping such as a **geophone**.

Harry Tate. The British R.E.8 biplane. R.E. stood for Reconnaissance Experimental. From rhyming slang, Harry Tate being a music-hall comedian.

Harry Tate's cavalry. The **Yeomanry**, the cavalry arm of the **terriers**.

Harver. The port of Le Havre (Lee Harver, or simply **Lee**), the most southerly of the cross-Channel routes used by the Army. **Tommy**'s French.

Hate. A regular, routine bombardment from **Jerry**'s artillery. The timing of his daily hates varied from sector to sector but often coincided with dawn and dusk. In September 1914, German newspapers published a song called 'The Hymn of Hate' by Ernst Lissauer, the chorus of which ran as follows: 'We will never forego our hate/ We have all but a single hate/ We love as one, we hate as one/ We have one foe and one alone – ENGLAND!' The song was an instant hit in **Blighty** and became a favourite of military bands on recruiting duty. Jerry prisoners were sometimes ordered to sing 'The Hymn of Hate' for their captors' entertainment.

'He wouldn't pull a soldier off his mother.' A jibe for a lazy comrade.

Heap. A disorderly soldier or **mob**. 'Here they come, mooching along, all of a heap!' was a welcoming sally offered to any tired squad returning to its **billet**.

Heavy. A big, powerful gun firing a heavy shell; heavy stuff.

Heavy Branch. See **Hush hush crowd**.

Heel Taps. See **Eat Apples**.

Hellfire Corner. A **hot spot** in **The Salient**, where a railway line crossed the Menin Road, the main artery supplying British forward **trenches**. The area within a 200-yard radius of this intersection was under constant **Jerry** bombardment for four years. Like many examples of **trench nomenclature**, Hellfire Corner started off as a nickname but became official when it appeared on military maps. See also, **Field Survey**.

High stepper. A smart, well-bred woman. From equitation. See also, **Filly**.

Hindenburg. Paul von Hindenburg, German Field Marshal. He became Chief of Staff in 1916 and remained the dominant personality in the High Command until the end of the war. As with **Kitchener**, one of his main assets was an unswerving public belief in his leadership.

Hindenburg Line. The line of **Jerry trenches**, **pill boxes** and tunnels started towards the end of 1916 after his drubbing on the Somme. In strictly military terms, the last two years on the **Western Front** was the story of how the **Allies** worked out how to tackle the Hindenburg Line. It was still under construction when it was breached by the 46th (North Midland) Division in September 1918, opening the way to victory.

Hipe. Rifle. **Regular Army** slang.

Hit the roof. To explode in anger, hitting one's head on the **dug-out** ceiling.

Hobnail express. To travel by foot. From the nails hammered into the soles of **daisies** to provide traction. See also, **Footslogger**.

'Holding the Line with a man and a boy.' Colloquial among **staff** officers to describe any thinly held sector or under-manned trench.

Holy Joe. A chaplain or pious sort. See also, **God botherer**, **Padre**, **Sky pilot**.

Hom forty. A freight wagon on a French train. **Tommy**'s French. Each wagon was painted with a notice – *Hommes 32–40, chevaux (en long) 8* – indicating that it had room for 40 men or eight horses. If the wooden floorboards were not copiously sprinkled with sand, the nags used to slide all over the place.

Hop over, hop the bags. To leave one's **trench** to attack. See also, **Jumping off line**.

'Hope it keeps fine for you . . .' A sympathetic valediction, especially for someone facing any imminent unpleasantness such as a **hop over**.

Hors de combat. An officer's phrase, straight from the French, meaning wounded, out of battle. Used colloquially to mean broken, useless or rejected in love.

Horlicks. A malted milk drink valued in food parcels. Colloquially, to make a horlicks of something was to make a bollocks of it, i.e. mess it up.

Horse length. Eight feet, the length of a horse. The length of a **donk** was set at six feet.

Horse valet. A sarcasm for a cavalryman or anyone grooming a horse.

Horse width. Three feet. The width of a **donk** was four feet.

Horsepower. Most horsepower in the **B.E.F.** at the start of the war was provided by horses rather than mechanised transport. The tonnage of **fodder** required was greater than the tonnage of ammunition required for the guns. More than 225,000 horses were killed during the war. See also, **Hairy**, **Pickled monkey**.

Hose. An **emma gee**, especially the lighter **Lewis gun**. See also, **Burst**, **Squirt**.

Hot, hot spot. Adjective for any dangerous place. See also, **Picnic**, **Warm**.

Hot cross bun. Ambulance. From the red cross on its side. See also, **Dhoolie wagon**.

Hot stuff (a bit of). Any non-professional female who might be enticed into going all the way sexually. Also, pornographic postcards.

Household Cavalry. The collective term for the most socially superior cavalry **regiments** – the Life Guards (red uniform jacket) and the Royal Horse Guards (blue uniform). Also known as the **Piccadilly Cowboys**.

Housewife. A cloth wrapper containing needles, cotton and various odds and ends for patching one's uniform. Pronounced hussif. It was part of a soldier's kit and had to be produced at inspection.

How, howitzer. An artillery piece for firing a heavy shell in an arc, thereby enabling it to hit targets screened by high ground. Howitzers were used particularly to destroy **trenches**, **dug-outs** and bunkers prior to a **show**. From the German, *howitz*, a medieval machine for hurling stones.

'How many times?' The ritual response to the news that a comrade had got married while on **leaf**. See also, **Flapper**, **Ring money**.

Howler. A very obvious and very silly mistake.

Hump. To lift or to carry. Also, to engage in **fornication**. Most infantrymen spent their time humping, but not in the sense they might have preferred. See also, **Roger**.

Hun. Individually, a **Jerry**. Collectively all Jerries. A British newspaper usage, derived from the policy of frightfulness applied by the Germans during their invasion of Belgium in August 1914. Thereafter the term Hun, often coupled with the adjective 'unspeakable', was revived whenever any new outrage needed to be reported. **Tommy** was less keen than his officers on Hun, preferring Jerry or **Fritz**. The original Huns were Tartar raiders who swept into Europe from West Asia in the fourth and fifth centuries, hence Hungary.

Hung up. To be hung up or to get hung up was to find one's progress blocked by barbed wire. **Artillery** fire and **Bangalore torpedoes** were meant to clear lanes in the enemy wire prior to an **infantry** attack, often with only partial success.

Hunter Bunter. Lieutenant-General Sir Aylmer Gould Hunter-Weston. Hunter Bunter got a bad case of sunstroke at **Jolly Polly** and some of his troops wondered if he was ever properly sane again. At the opening of the Somme offensive, 1 July 1916, his VIII Corps suffered a higher proportion of casualties than any other formation for no gain of ground whatsoever.

Huntley and Palmer. The paired set of **Lewis guns** on a British warplane. Huntley and Palmer was a well-known firm of biscuit makers.

'Hurry up and wait!' A sarcastic phrase for the Army's general way of doing things.

Hussar. A light cavalryman. From the Hungarian for twenty, *usz*. Only one in twenty applicants was deemed worthy of acceptance.

Hush hush. Army adjective denoting something secret or confidential.

Hush hush crowd. The collective noun for the first groups of men to train to fight in **tanks**. They were given the official name **Heavy Branch**, Machine Gun Corps to disguise the real nature of their work.

Hutment. An encampment with huts instead of tents. A feature of the **base** and **rest**.

Hypo helmet. A hood made of flannel which, when soaked in a chemical solution known as hypo, was the first proper British gas mask. See also, **'Goggle-eyed bugger with the tit.'**

IS FOR

INDIAN

'C' Company, 5th West Kent Fusiliers,
British Expeditionary Force,
4th September, 1915.

Dear Edward,

   We have moved again. The gilded staff, God bless
'em, are lining up their pieces for their opening
gambit. I am not allowed to tell you where we are
billeted, in case a Jerry spy is reading this over
your shoulder, but it is such a horrible irony I
cannot resist the temptation – six farms and
a couple of cottages called Paradis. The men
have naturally translated it as Paradise, which
it is anything but. Our ever-faithful Jocks are
alongside but the Brigade has also been given a
couple of Indian battalions to take care of and
one of them has been attached to us for training.
Colonel Rickett, of course, is in his element,
although it turns out that this lot are from the
Northwest Frontier, while his former regiment
was down in Bombay, a completely different kettle
of fish. Still, most of the officers are English
and we seem to be getting on quite well so far.
Nothing marks out an Old Sweat more than the
quantity of Hindoo in his slang so we have been
slinging the bat for all we are worth. Yesterday, as
I was parading a fatigue in Paradise's only street,
prior to some necessary humping for the gunners,

an Indian ration party came along. Naturally, the men were keen to display their linguistic sophistication.

'Oi, Indi-boy! Mustafa! Arsty, arsty! Me mucho booka. You got any chinni or bung going spare?' The naik in charge groped for a suitable reply but having been recently in the company of Jocks the purity of his backchat was somewhat tainted. 'Alleyman no bon,' he blurted out. 'Me like King Jarge bloody good. Tik hai, Johnny! Up yours! F——this for a game of soldiers!' That little exchange kept the lads amused all night. The chorus, 'Tik hai, Johnny! Up yours!' greeted every bit of interference Jerry sent in our direction. We're a happy bunch so long as there are enough fags and swear words to go round.

Yours as ever,

Chazzer

I., I-Branch. Military Intelligence. The job of Intelligence officers was to gather information about the enemy's strength and intentions, mainly by intercepting his communications, questioning prisoners and scrutinising aerial photographs. Intelligence officers were usually given the badge of the Royal Fusiliers to wear on their uniforms and were known as green tabs from the colour of their **gorgets**.

'I have no pain, dear mother, but oh I am so dry . . .' A drinker's catchphrase, the tag line being, '. . . Lead me to the brewery and lay me down to die.'

'I want three volunteers – you, you and you!' A formula favoured by **N.C.O.**s to raise the required manpower for a **fatigue**. See also, **'Kitchener wants *you*!'**

Iddy umpty. A **signaller**. From **Morse code**, which translated the letters of the alphabet into electrical impulses – dots and dashes – that could be transmitted along a copper wire. In training signallers, the words **iddy** and **umpty** were used for a dot or a dash when it was tapped out on a buzzer. See also, **Buzz**.

Ident, indent. An Army requisition form. More generally, throughout the Army, any necessary piece of military documentation. See also, **Bumf**, **Chit (1)**, **Ticket**.

Identity disc. A metal or fibre token stamped with a soldier's name, his **regimental number**, and religion. Later in the war, two discs were worn; one red, the other green. If a man was killed, the red disc was returned to his unit with his personal effects while the green disc stayed on his body. This was his **cold meat ticket**. Men who did not like to wear their discs around the wrist or neck might hitch them to the braces of their trousers.

'If it keeps on like this, someone's going to get hurt.' A sarcasm sometimes heard amid the din of an intense **barrage**.

'If we had some eggs we could have egg and bacon. If we had some bacon.' A phrase deployed with bitter longing by men with nothing to eat.

Improperly dressed. To make a mistake in wearing one's uniform. Having a button undone without permission was a **crime**.

Incinerator. Portable device for burning **latrine** waste and any scraps from the cookhouse not deemed suitable for **salvage**. When **Tommy** wasn't constipated he was calculated to produce an average of 4.5 ounces of excrement and 8 ounces of urine per day. Incinerators were a particular feature of camps and **billets** in **rest** areas.

Indent. See **Ident**.

Infantry. See **P.B.I.**

Ink slinger. A clerk in uniform, a **pen pusher**. Also, a journalist attached to the Army as an official correspondent. He was given an officer's uniform and a green armband for his sleeve. The most popular English newspaper on the **Western Front** was the *Daily Mirror* because of its photographs.

Inky Bill. Major-General Edward Ingouville-Williams, commander of the 34th Division. On 22 July 1916 Inky Bill was making a personal reconnaissance of the battlefield near Mametz Wood when he was killed by a shell fragment.

Interval. The gap, measured in time or distance, between men on the march. See **Footslogger**.

Iodine lancers. Generic for medics, **dhoolie wallahs**, **Fannys**, etc.

Ips. Another name for Ypres. Same as **Eeps**, Weeps, **Wipers**.

Iron cross. The **Jerry** gallantry medal, a black cross on a black and white ribbon. There were two classes. About 5,000,000 iron crosses of the second class were issued during the war and 218,000 of the first class.

Iron footed bastards. The East Yorkshire Regiment, credited with prodigies of **footslogging** – 80 miles in one day – during their service in the Empire.

Iron ration. A tinned meal and four **dog** biscuits. A soldier was not permitted to eat his iron ration without an order. Colloquially, iron rations referred to heavy shell fire. From the German *eiserne portion*, rations in a metal case.

Issue. Army verb meaning to supply. The **quarter-bloke** never gave out stores, he **issued** them. Any item provided by the Army was therefore an issue. As such, it was associated with the commonplace, the basic, the ordinary. Hence the following exchange: 'Got any decent **fags** on you?' 'Sorry, chum. Only issue.' Issue was endlessly applicable. Mud, bad weather and shellfire might all be described as issue. To say of a comrade that he had 'got his issue' meant he had received his ration from Quartermaster Death.

'It came off in my hand.' The soldier's stock excuse when accused of breaking something. Another line of defence was, 'It was already broke when they issued it.' See also, **'Destroyed by shellfire.'**

Itch. Generally, to have the itch was to feel the activity of **chats** about one's person. Specifically, it meant infestation by the scabies parasite.

'It's a game!' The weary assertion that the war didn't make sense, except to those military professionals who were advancing their careers by running it.

Ivan. A Russian, the Russians. The equivalent of **Tommy** and **Jerry**.

I.W.T., Inland Water Transport. The Army barge service, established 1915. Hospital barges were used to evacuate the wounded to **bases** like Rouen, **Ruin**, on the River Seine. Rafts of barges also transported stores across the **Drink**, especially bulky cargoes like **fodder**.

IS FOR

JOY
SPOT

'C' Company, 5th West Kent Fusiliers,
British Expeditionary Force,
12th September, 1915.

Dearest Mudge,

I think I have done rather well, given the
distractions of the campaign, to remember your
birthday. I hope the enclosed genuine souvenir of
the battle zone reaches you in time for the happy
day. It is rather too sentimental, I know, but it
is one of the few delicate, light things one can buy
out here and it says exactly what I mean. I will
certainly be thinking of you because I know your
main thoughts these days are of me and the Hun-
ish peril. Console yourself that I am ensconced in
a very safe place right now. At least half of the
nearest town is still standing and there are even
women and children there, so there is more than a
semblance of what might be called normal life. As
I was leaving a tea shop, having gorged myself on
pastries to the point of sickness, I almost bumped
into the Prince of Wales. He is out here on the
staff of a Guards brigade, I think. He looked the
perfect chocolate soldier, all spick and span in his
immaculate uniform, with a brass hat alongside
to keep him out of mischief. He is incredibly boyish
looking and evidently enjoys being the centre
of attention. You can tell Mrs Blundell that he

graciously returned my salute, which means I am almost certain to be promoted. That should take the wind out of her sails the next time she starts boasting about her precious Willie. Honestly, his being in the <u>Lancers</u> makes him no safer than anyone else. The <u>donkey wallopers</u> have all had their nags taken away and do their turn in the mud and slime like the rest of us.

Many happy returns, you dear old thing, and do try to stop worrying so much. I am simply not ready yet to quit this ball of clay. There is plenty more fighting to be done before <u>Jerry</u> comes to his senses but what you must try to understand is that I am not out here on my own. I am part of a large and bloodthirsty army which is quite capable of looking after itself and teaching the Hun a sound lesson into the bargain.

Many happy returns of the day,
your ever-loving son,

Charlie

Jab. A medical inoculation delivered through a needle. The anti-tetanus jab to stop lockjaw was the most common inoculation on the battlefield.

Jack Johnson. Any heavy **Jerry** shell but especially one from the powerful 5.9 **how**. It burst with a mighty **concussion** and a thick cloud of black smoke. The American boxer, the original Jack Johnson, also known as the Galveston Giant, was the first black heavyweight champion of the world. He held the world title from 1908–15. See also, **Great White Hope**, **Woolly Bear**.

Jacks. Military police, the **red caps**.

Jag. A drinking bout.

Jakes. Lavatory. See also, **Latrine**.

Jam. Good, a term of approval. The word jam was never used to mean the sweet fruity confection spread on bread; that was **pozzie** or **paint**.

Jam jar. A German mortar bomb. See also, **Minnie**, **Sausage**.

'Jam on it.' An expression meaning exceptionally nice. Any **cushy** job was said to come with jam on it.

Jam stealers. The Army Service Corps, **A.S.C., Ally Sloper's Cavalry**.

Jam tin. An improvised **bomb** first seen during the winter of 1914–15 and fired from a catapult to increase its range. It was a tin can filled with scrap iron, a wad of explosive and a rudimentary fuse. See also, **Stink pot**.

Jankers King. An **N.C.O.** in the **red caps**, the provost sergeant.

Jankers men. Defaulters, those put on jankers, punishment duties.

Jannack. Honest, straight. From dialect.

Japan. Bread. **Tommy**'s French. *Du pain*, bread, became *dupang* in

Frahnsay, hence japan in trench lingo. It was a particular usage of the **Kitchener** volunteers. **Rooty** remained the **Regular Army**'s word for bread.

Jaw. To talk. See also, **Pi jaw**.

Jerk. A spurt of effort or energy. To do something with a jerk was to do it quickly. To do something with an extra jerk was to do it very quickly. 'Put a jerk in it!' See also, **Jildy**.

Jerry. A German or, collectively, the Germans. **Tommy**'s preferred name for his enemy. The French preferred **Fritz**.

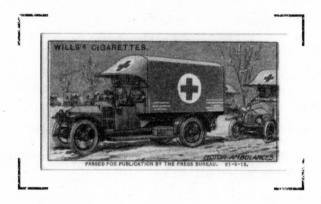

Jiggy-jig, jig-a-jig. See **Fornication**, **Jump**, **Red Lamp**.

Jildy. Effort, energy. From the Hindustani **juldi**, quick, hurry up. The opposite of **arsty**. See also, **Ginger up**.

Jingo. A blusteringly patriotic person.

Jock. A Scottish soldier. If the Jock was also a Highlander he wore a kilt instead of trousers; shoes and gaiters instead of boots; a **split-arse cap** instead of the **forage cap** worn by the rest of the Army. Any man in a Scottish **regiment** was a Jock, regardless of nationality.

Joffre. The French Commander-in-Chief from the start of the war until December 1916. Joseph Joffre was legendary for never skipping lunch, hence the rotundity which earned him the nickname Papa.

Jollop. Army tea laced with a **bromide**.

Jolly Polly. Vernacular for Gallipoli.

Joss. Luck. Also, any foreign religion or superstition. From the Asiatic pronunciation of the Portuguese *deos*, god. A joss house was any place of worship.

Joy ride. A trip taken for personal pleasure by horse, plane or car.

Joy spot. The destination of a **joy ride**, a place behind the lines preserving some of the most precious amenities of civilisation such as table linen and clean glasses. An officers' phrase.

Ju ju. Army slang for superstition. African derivation. See also, **Joss**.

Jump. A free ride in a lorry. Also, the act of sexual intercourse.

'Jump to it!' Do it now! Often heard after the issue of an order by an N.C.O.

Jumping off line. The **trench**(es) from where an attack or patrol was launched; it was not always the front line.

IS FOR

KITCHENAIRE

'C' Company, 5th West Kent Fusiliers,
British Expeditionary Force,
18th September, 1915.

Dear Edward,

The most embarrassing thing has happened and
I blame you for <u>blowing the gaff</u>. You told M & F,
didn't you, that I had been wounded? There can be
no other explanation for what happened yesterday,
when a runner arrived from <u>Brigade</u> asking me
to report urgently in person. I was taken straight
to the resident <u>green tab</u> who asked if I might have
inadvertently given away military information of
use to the enemy. This most serious accusation I
denied with vehement innocence whereupon he took me
out to the stables where was displayed a small crate,
addressed to me in Mudge's fair hand. It had fallen
off the post cart and had been handed in by a local
who had demanded five francs for his trouble. Inside
this crate was a pangolin, one of those frightful
armoured vests one sees advertised in the classified
sections of the weekly magazines. I was utterly
mortified and disgusted. Anyone caught wearing
one of these ridiculous outfits is immediately labelled
<u>windy</u> and no-one with an ounce of spunk would be
seen dead in one.

The look on my face must have convinced
<u>I-Branch</u> that I was, indeed, the innocent victim

of an overly anxious mother's protective instincts. Apparently a routine general order has been sent out to check on officers receiving body armour – in case they have been using their <u>sticky jacks</u> to speak too freely of what is intended in the very near future. It is certainly the case, in <u>trenches</u>, that <u>Jerry</u> seems to guess with annoying foresight what we are up to.

As for the wretched pangolin, it was nothing more than a canvas waistcoat with flimsy metal scales stitched to it. As armour plating, of course, it was totally useless. We took it out into the field for some <u>buckshee</u> target practice and at a range of 50 yards a bullet went through it like a knife through butter. However, the shot-up crate will come in handy as we are always short of kindling out here. You are under sworn oath not to let out a word of this to anyone. I will conduct my own investigations in person, should the promised spot of leave come my way, which I am hoping it will. Not a word about that either. If it does come through I want it to be a pleasant surprise for the oldies.

Love to the nephers and kneesers as ever,
your bro',

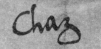

P.S. I enclose fag cards for the nephers and lace postcards for the kneesers. Rather sweet aren't they?

K1. The designation for the first 100,000 men to respond to Lord **Kitchener**'s call for volunteers in 1914. K1 was followed by K2, K3 and so on. See also, **New Army**.

Kaiser. The Emperor of Germany and King of Prussia, Wilhelm II, grandson of Queen Victoria. From the Latin name Caesar, taken by the Teutonic tribes to mean emperor. As Commander-in-Chief of the German Army Kaiser Bill spent the war in uniform but came to have less and less influence. See also, **Big Willie**.

Kaiser Bill's birthday. A term of derision for any seemingly pointless and otherwise inexplicable offensive action by the Germans.

Kaiser's Oak. A tree standing within German lines at Gommecourt on the Somme battlefield, which marked the point of **Jerry**'s furthest westward penetration into France.

Kamerad. The **Jerry** word of surrender, meaning comrade. See also, **'Kinder I haf.'**

Kaput. Broken, finished, dead. German derivation. See also, **Napoo**.

Keating's powder. An insecticide for killing **chats** and other vermin. Made from the garden flower, pyrethrum. 'Keating's powder does the trick/ Kills all bugs and fleas off quick/ Keating he's a jolly brick/ Bravo! Long live Keating!' See also, **Vermijelli**.

'Keep your bowels open and your mouth shut.' The **Old Sweat**'s recipe for a successful military career.

'Keeping the fire warm?' A sarcasm directed at one hogging the heat.

Kellner. A surname associated with **Jerry** waiters in London's pre-war restaurants and used in the trenches as a disparagement. See also, **'Waiter!'**

Khaki. The colour of the British Army uniform. From the Urdu *khaki*, dust-coloured. First worn on the Afghan frontier, 1848, and adopted as the British field uniform during the Boer War, 1899–1902. See also, *Feldgrau*.

Kilo. Abbreviation for kilometre, as seen on French signposts. By the end of the war the **A.S.C.** had adopted the kilo as its standard measure of distance while the **P.B.I.** kept to the mile. Compare the **Jerry** nickname for infantryman, *kilometerfesser*, kilometre eater.

'Kinder I haf.' A **Jerry**'s appeal for mercy, on the grounds of having children.

Kindermorde. The German word for the slaughter of thousands of young **Jerries**, many of them university students, in the early campaign in Flanders. The term was especially applied to those killed in the first attempts to take **Eeps** in 1915.

WILLS'S CIGARETTES.

GENERAL IVANOFF.

Kindness. Sex slang. The average **Tommy**'s idea of doing a kindness to a woman was to provide her with sexual intercourse. See also, **Fornication**, **Hump**, **Jiggy-jig**, **Jump**, **Roger**.

King's birthday. Pay day. See also, **Kaiser Bill's birthday**.

King's Pledge. The patriotic announcement by George V that he was giving up alcohol for the **duration**, as an example to right-minded subjects.

King's shilling. The nominal sum given to each recruit on joining the Army. One popular recruiting song, 'I'll Make A Man Of You', usually rendered by a buxom woman, contained the promise, 'And on Saturday I'm willing/ If you'll only take the shilling/ To make a man of any man of you.'

Kip. Sleep, to sleep. Also, a bed, board, hole or pile of straw arranged for sleep.

Kirchner. Raphael Kirchner was an Austrian artist specialising in delicately erotic depictions of sparsely clad females – Kirchner girls. His work reached the **Western Front** via the French magazine *La Vie Parisienne* and the London *Sketch*, which published his pictures as double-page pull-outs.

Kirchnerise. To decorate a **dug-out** or **billet** with **Kirchner** girls.

'Kiss me, sergeant.' Sarcastic response to a **sergeant**'s goodnight, after reading the orders for the following day.

Kit inspection. The inspection of a soldier's entire kit, in which each item was laid out in prescribed order on his groundsheet or blanket. Any item found to be missing had to be replaced at his own expense, hence the prevalence of **scrounging**.

Kitchenaire. The French pronunciation of **Kitchener**.

Kitchener man, Kitch. One who responded to **Kitchener**'s call, a civilian in uniform, a Kitch.

Kitchener of Khartoum, Lord, K-of-K. The general who was made War Minister in August 1914. Kitchener saw early on that it was going to be a long war and set about raising the armies that would be needed to win it. As a leader, he found it difficult to delegate and he irritated **War House** colleagues by interfering in detail, hence K-of-Chaos. His high public standing contributed to the success of the famous recruiting poster, 'Your country needs – YOU.' Kitchener was drowned at sea, 16 June 1916, while on his way to Russia.

'Kitchener wants you!' A satirical parody addressed to anyone selected by an **N.C.O.** for a dangerous or unpleasant **fatigue**. See also, **'I want three volunteers . . .'**

Kitchener's Army, Kitchener's Mob. The collective term for those who joined up in response to **Kitchener**'s appeal for volunteers in 1914, the **New Armies**. It took months to get them trained and equipped. The first **Kitchener men** to get to the **Western Front**, the 9th (Scottish) Division, didn't arrive until 9 May 1915. Many officers of the **Regular Army** felt unable to accept their Kitchener comrades as equals, they were merely amateurs.

Kite. An aeroplane, a contraption of wood and string floating in the air.

Kiwi. A mechanic in the **Royal Flying Corps**. From the flightless bird of New Zealand. Kiwi was also a brand of shoe polish, hence the nickname Kiwi King for any officer or **N.C.O.** punctilious about appearances.

Knee drill. See **Church parade**.

Knife. The British **bayonet**, all seventeen inches of it. In **trenches** the knife was mostly used domestically – as clothes hook, crowbar, can opener, **toasting fork** or candle holder.

Knobkerry. A studded, wooden cosh for use in **trench** raids. African derivation.

Knock off. Steal. Also, to finish work. Knocking-off time was the time set for the end of a patrol or **fatigue**.

Knocked for six. To be killed or badly wounded. Also, to defeat someone in an argument, to floor him with a nasty surprise. Cricketing derivation. From the sinking sensation felt by a bowler on seeing his delivery lofted over the boundary. See also, **Open the bowling**.

Knocking about. Idle, at rest, loitering. Soldiers without a specific duty to perform were said to be knocking about. Unguarded stores or someone else's kit were fair game for **knocking off** if no one was looking. A knocking shop was a brothel. To knock up a mam'selle was to make her pregnant.

Knockaloe. A detention camp on the Isle of Man for interned Germans and others categorised as undesirable aliens. There were similar camps on the British mainland. See also, **Maggi soup**.

Knut, nut. A dandy, any **temporary gentleman** showing too keen an interest in his appearance, perhaps by slipping some **bunce** to the **dersie** to make discreetly fashionable adjustments to his uniform. Knut came from a popular song – 'I'm Gilbert, the Filbert, the Knut with a K' – performed by an actor called Basil Hallam, who served as an **observer** in the **Royal Flying Corps**. Hallam was killed, 20 August 1916, after falling from a **sausage** without his **brolly**.

Koepenik. A military impostor. In 1906, in Germany, a small-time thief and conman called Wilhelm Voigt was able to pass himself off as an army captain by virtue of a second-hand uniform. He tricked several genuine soldiers into following his orders and ended up robbing the town hall of Koepenick. Once the affair had been reported in the press, 'Captain Koepenik' became a byword for any military impostor. Before the war, there was a waxwork of him in Madame Tussaud's museum in London.

Kosher. Pure, acceptable, the real thing. Cockney borrowing from **Yiddish**.

Kultur. The collective word for those ideas taken by **Jerry** to signify progress in politics, economics and the arts. The word was used sarcastically to ridicule militarism, aggression and the un-English subordination of individual liberty to the authority of the state.

L

IS FOR

LAST
POST

'C' Company, 5th West Kent Fusiliers,
British Expeditionary Force,
21st September, 1915.

Dear David,

Thank you very much for your letter. You are
most welcome to the cigarette cards. There are
plenty out here. I might send you some more if
you write to me again. You are the first of my
nephews or kneesers to write since I got here,
despite my pleas. You are now my favourite.
Please find enclosed a postal order for the sum of
half a crown. All of it is to be spent in the tuck
shop. None of it is to be spent on your brothers or
sisters. They can have their own postal orders. All
they have to do is pick up a pen, dip it in ink and
cover a whole page with nonsense. I would answer
your questions one by one if I had the time but
it would feel like sitting an examination. Also,
I do think it rather a cheat to write a letter that
is mostly questions when what I crave is news of
your own doings, how you are faring at school, how
the cricket ended up, etcetera.

You did ask one question I feel I must
address and the answer is – No, I do not hate the
Jerries. I think, in general, they are a rather
beastly set and they did a very wrong thing
starting this war, for which they must be punished.

But hate is not what I feel. Nor do I think any of my <u>Tommies</u> hate Jerry. We are too close to him. We sit in our <u>trench</u> behind our barbed <u>wire</u> and he sits in his trench behind his wire and although we shoot at each other and throw <u>bombs</u> from time to time that is not because we hate each other but because that is the game we are playing. It his big <u>guns</u> we hate. When the heavy stuff is flying overhead, poor old Jerry is the same as us. We squat down and hope for the best.

Please write to me again if you have time. There should be some good news rather soon that should buck us all up. I hope so.

Best of regards, old lad, and stick at the Latin. It will be worth it in the end.

Your very best uncle,

Charlie

Labour Corps. Formed in 1917 to provided a command structure for the Army's labour, i.e. the **infantry**'s **pioneers**; the drivers and mechanics of the **A.S.C.**; prisoners-of-war serving as labour; and various **salvage** units. The Labour Corps grew to contain nearly 200,000 men. Their badge was a pick and shovel crossed with a rifle.

Labour forces. Correct jargon for foreign labour used as non-military manpower. More than 130,000 Chinese, Egyptian, Indian and African labourers served in France. Their contracts said they were not to be deployed within ten miles of the front line.

Ladies from hell. Men in kilts, the **Jocks**. So named by **Jerry**'s newspapers.

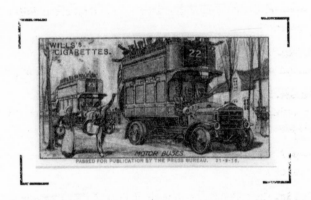

Lady of the Limp. A statue of the Madonna and Child on the basilica of the French town of Albert, the ruins of which stood in the same relationship to the Somme battlefield as Ypres to **The Salient**. The statue was knocked sideways by a shell, 15 July 1915, but engineers tied her feet fast with cables and she stayed at an awkward, diving angle for over two years. Army **joss** held that only when the Virgin fell would the war end. She was knocked down by British **artillery** in March 1918, but the war went on. She was also known as the Hanging Madonna, **Golden Virgin** and Leaning Virgin.

Lamps. The eyes.

Lance jack. A lance corporal. As the lowest rank of **N.C.O.**, with one **stripe** on his sleeve, the main job of the lance corporal was to supervise **fatigues**. From the Italian *lancia-spezzata*, broken lance, a trooper who, having lost his lance or horse in action, had to serve on foot while being re-armed or re-mounted. See also, **Chevron**, **Corp**, **Troop**.

Lancer. A cavalryman armed with a lance. The German equivalent was *uhlan*, who was heard much of in the early days before **trench** warfare made cavalry obsolete as a means of reconnaissance. **Jerry**'s slang for *uhlan* was lamp-lighter.

Landowner. A comrade in his grave. See also, **Rest camp**, **Stiff's paddock**.

Landship. Code word for the **tank** during its secret development in England and subsequent export to France. See also, **Hush hush**.

Language. Swearing, coarseness or obscenity. Apart from its decorative function in conversation, profanity was considered a necessity in getting things across to the **Other Ranks**.

Lash-up. A botched attack or **stunt**. To lash up something was to make a mess of it.

Last lot in. The collective noun used on the **relief** of a **trench** to refer to its previous occupants. The qualities attributed to the last lot in were rarely complimentary.

Last Post. The bugle call to signify the end of each day's work, when all men had to be in camp. It was also the symbolic last farewell at a soldier's funeral, after which followed **Reveille**, the wake-up call.

Latrine. Army jargon for lavatory, usually a bucket or a pole suspended over a pit. From the *Latin* latrina. The latrine **sap** was a known **hot spot** because in aerial photographs it looked like a mortar or machine gun post and was therefore interesting to the enemy.

Latrine rumour. Gossip or news of dubious veracity. **Gup** was also available at such regular meeting places as the **canteen**, dump or **estaminy**. **Jerry**'s word for latrine was *latrinen*, whence emanated their *latrinen-parole*, latrine passwords, *latrinen-gerucht*, latrine rumours and *latrinen-befehl*, latrine orders.

Lay on. To arrange, provide or organise.

Leaf. The correct pronunciation for a period of **leave**.

'Lean on your chinstraps, lads!' A call to rally marching troops as they approached a hill or gradient. See also, **Chinstrap**.

Leave. The period of time when a soldier was authorised to be off duty and away from the war. Leave came round rarely for men, more often for officers. If a **private** got more than ten days leave in a year he was doing very well. The period of leave began the moment a man left his unit and included all travelling time to and from **Blighty**. Men going on leave had to take their rifle and kit with them.

Leap frog, leap frogging. A method of attack by waves of **infantry** in conjunction with a **creeping barrage**. The first objective having been attained, troops would **dig in** or consolidate and the following wave would leap frog over them to attack **Jerry**'s next line and the next until the final objective was reached.

Lee. See **Harver**.

Lee Enfield. The British **infantry** rifle. It fired a .303 cartridge, either singly or from a magazine holding ten of them. Named after its designer, James Paris Lee, and the place where it was made, the London suburb of Enfield, home of the Royal Small Arms Factory. In **trenches**, rifles were inspected twice a day, morning and evening. See also, **Hipe**.

Left hand man. The sentry furthest to the left. One sentry was the furthest left of the whole Army and he was known as the left hand man of the **Line**.

Leg it. To run away. See also, **'Alley!'**

Lemonade wallah. A teetotaller.

'Let's be having you!' An **N.C.O.**'s shout to rouse men for a **parade** or **fatigue**.

Lewis gun. A light **emma gee** named after its American inventor, Colonel Isaac Lewis. It fired bullets from a flat, circular magazine called a **pan** or **drum**. After firing about twelve of these drums, the average Lewis would become so hot it would seize up.

Lieutenant. The lowest rank of officer in the British Army, a second lieutenant being junior to a lieutenant. From the Latin *locum teneris*, place holder, i.e. in place of a **captain**. See also, **Pip**, **Subaltern**, **Temporary gentleman**.

Life preserver. A cosh, for use in a **trench** raid, perhaps a **knobkerry**.

Lift. To steal. See also, **Scrounge**.

Light duties. The medicine prescribed for a sick man by the **M.O.** if he wasn't sick enough for hospital. Light duties meant **fatigues**, peeling potatoes, emptying the **latrine** buckets, etc. See also, **Number nine pill**.

Lights Out. The last bugle call of the day. See also, **Last Post**.

'Like a bag of shit (tied up with string).' An **N.C.O.**'s comment on a badly turned-out soldier. Also, the correct term for an officer sitting awkwardly on his **charger**.

Limber. A two-wheeled attachment to a gun carriage for carrying **ammo**. It was positioned between the team of horses and the gun itself.

Lime Light. A signalling device. It produced a bright beam of light by passing oxygen through a flame onto a pencil length of lime that burned to white-hot intensity. A shutter was used to break the beam into **Morse code**.

Line, the. The opposing **trench** systems, the battle zone, the actual **Western Front**. But Line was also used equally often to refer to the lines of communication behind the trenches, i.e. the supply and evacuation routes between the **Front** and the **base**.

Lingo. Language, especially as spoken by a foreigner. From Latin *lingua*. See also, **Frahnsay**, **Sling the bat**.

Linseed Lancers. The **R.A.M.C.**, **Royal Army Medical Corps**. See also, **Castor Oil Dragoons**.

Lip. Answering back to a superior. A **crime**. See also, **Dumb insolence**.

Listening post. A shell crater or **sap**-head used for keeping tabs on the enemy. The listeners would be relieved every couple of hours. See also, **Earwig**, **Harker**.

Little Willie. The **Kaiser**'s son, Crown Prince Wilhelm. He commanded first an army (the German Fifth Army) during the invasion of Belgium and then a group of armies during the German offensive at Verdun, 1916. Little Willie was also the code name given to Britain's first prototype **tank**.

Live one. Weapons were live when loaded and ready to fire. Ammunition was live when primed and ready to explode. 'Careful with that, lad, it's a live one.'

Livestock. Lice, vermin. See also, **Chat**.

Lobster. An articulated, three-piece item of **Jerry** body armour, *infantrie-panzer*, introduced during 1916. It was attached to the front torso by **webbing**. A Jerry crouched in a shell hole could switch it round to his back to fend off **shrapnel**.

London Gazette. See **Gazette**.

London Irish. A territorial regiment raised from **Micks** living in London, officially designated the 18th Battalion, the London Regiment, London Irish Rifles. Men of the Irish Rifles were among those who kicked footballs in front of them as they attacked at Loos, 25 September 1915. See also, **Terrier**.

Look in. A share of something. When a man received a parcel from home he would offer his muckers a look in on its contents. See also, **Muck in**.

Looking stick. Telescope or trench periscope. See also, **Field glass**, **Perisher**.

Loose wallah. Thief. From the Hindustani *lus*, thief.

Loot. To steal. From the Hindustani *lut*, theft.

Lost. The adjective for any shell or bomb which, having departed, was not seen to arrive.

Louse trap. A jerkin of goatskin or sheepskin issued as winter uniform. Because it kept men warm, it encouraged the activities of **chats**.

Lovat Scouts. A Scottish **regiment** raised in 1900 by Simon Fraser, Lord Lovat, consisting mainly of Highland gamekeepers and stalkers. On the **Western Front** they were used as specialist **snipers** and **observers**.

Loyal ill discipline. Riotous misbehaviour that fell short of armed mutiny. There were riots at **Eat Apples** and other **bases** but nothing in the British Army like the French mutinies of May and June 1917, when whole battalions of **Frogs** quit their **trenches** and order was restored by the imposition of exemplary executions.

Lucifer. A match, for lighting a **fag**. See also, **Asquiths**.

Lucky one. A fortunate wound in an unembarrassing part of the anatomy that required evacuation to **Blighty**.

'Lump into it!' Do it with energy. Cockney derivation. See also, **Jerk**, **Jildy**.

IS FOR

MASCOT

'C' Company, 5ᵗʰ West Kent Fusiliers,
British Expeditionary Force,
22ⁿᵈ September, 1915.

Dear Edward,

The enclosed sealed envelope contains my last
message to M & F, to be given to them in the
event of my death but not before that event has
been confirmed beyond doubt. All we have been
working towards for the past few weeks is about
to come off and it is only right to take a realistic
view of one's prospects. Tomorrow we move into
position for <u>Zero</u>. Our <u>brigade</u> is not in the main
<u>push</u> but out on the left <u>flank</u>. Our job is to
distract <u>Jerry</u> and pin him down so he can't make a
nuisance of himself elsewhere. There will be a hard
fight but no glory. There is very little of that in
this war, just the satisfaction of doing one's duty.
Thank you, by the way, for bringing pressure to
bear on the dear old nephers and kneesers. It did
put some <u>ginger</u> into me to find a letter from
David in my last sheaf. He is what I am fighting
for. And Daphne and Vickie and Teddy. The world
would be an intolerable place for them to grow
up in (and you to grow old in) if <u>Kultur</u> were to
triumph. I will be taking D's letter into battle.
I am not afraid to die. I have been re-reading
my Meditations these past few days. 'Man, you

have been a citizen in this world city, what does it matter whether for five years or fifty?' Not afraid to go, but afraid to linger, of being horribly wounded and maimed for life. My prayer to the gods is that I come through in one piece. If I am <u>to get it in the neck</u>, I want it quick and clean and not in the <u>orchestra.</u>

If this is to be my last word, Eddie, I want you to know that I go willingly, in gratitude for all England has given me, including everything Cartwright.

With respect and affection,
your brother for ever,

Charles, Charlie-boy, Chazzers

Mac, macintosh. A waterproof trench coat. From the Scottish manufacturer Macintosh, who was the first (1824) to successfully rubberise fabric.

Maconachie. A tinned meal of meat and vegetables, branded with the name of its Scottish manufacturer. Preferred by many to the ubiquitous **bully**.

Mad minute. A burst of rapid fire from every available rifle. The proficient rifleman was expected to fire at least fifteen **rounds** per minute.

'Mafeesh!' Finished! No more! Gone! From Arabic. See also, **Makoo**, **Napoo**.

Maffick. To celebrate with rowdiness. Derived from the riotous scenes in London that marked the relief of Mafeking during the Boer War, 17 May 1900. A similar Saturnalia was repeated in London on Armistice Day, 11 November 1918.

Maggi soup. A brand of packet soup produced by a Swiss-German firm. During the spy mania in **Blighty** during 1914, it was erroneously reported that advertising signs for Maggi soup were being used by **Jerry** agents to send messages to each other.

'Mail up!' The post-**wallah**'s announcement of his arrival. At its peak, the Army was handling some 12,500,000 letters and 800,000 parcels, per week. A temporary parcels office set up in Regent's Park, London, covered more than five acres.

Major. An officer ranking between a **captain** and a lieutenant colonel. His badge was a crown. Major was also slang for a **sergeant major**, and the crown in **Crown and Anchor**.

Make. To steal.

'Make it yourself?' The inevitable disparagement on being presented with an amateur-looking **box of tricks**.

'Make way for the Woolwich Arsenal!' A bystander's ironic greeting for a rival **infantry mob** passing through in full marching order. The first arsenal in England was built at the Royal Dockyard, Woolwich, whence the famous London football team.

Makings. The necessary ingredients for anything, e.g. tea leaves and **dooly** for a **brew**, papers and tobacco for rolling **fags**.

Makoo. None, out of stock, all gone. See also, **'Mafeesh!'**, **Napoo**.

Malinger. To try to avoid duty by feigning the symptoms of plague or pox. A soldier bent on this end was a malingerer. See also, **Dodge the column**, **Swing the lead**.

Mangle. An **emma gee**. From the domestic appliance for wringing wet laundry between two hand-cranked rollers. Compare the German *nuhmaschine*, sewing machine, and the French *moulin de café*, coffee grinder. From mangonel, a medieval siege machine for catapulting projectiles at the enemy, from the Greek *manganon*, engine of war.

Manjee, monjay. Food. Also, to eat. **Tommy**'s French. From *manger*, to eat.

Manjee wallah. A cook.

Marksman. An accurate shot with the rifle, a sharpshooter. The marksman differed from the **sniper** by remaining an integral part of his **platoon**. See also, **Dabster**.

Mascot. A personal keepsake to invoke protection. It was most usually a ring, button or badge but there was also a craze for adopting animals as **battalion** mascots. Canadians and South Africans brought all sorts of beasts with them, including wolves and bears. London Zoo found itself with scores of extra mouths to feed when these units finished their training in England and crossed to France.

Matlow. A sailor. From the French *matelot*, sailor. See also, **Bugger**.

M.C., Military Cross. The **gallantry** medal for **captains** and
lieutenants instituted in December 1914, a silver cross on a purple
and white ribbon. Known disparagingly as the **Maconachie** Cross
because it came up with the rations.

Meat ticket. See **Identity disc**.

Meatless day. A **Blighty** phrase for any day on which a civilian
had to go without meat as an economy measure. Meatless days were
voluntary at first but food shortages during 1917 made them a
regular feature. By 1918, Londoners were having two meatless days
per week.

Medicine and duty. The number nine in **Bingo**. See **Number Nine
pill**.

Menin Road meat extract. Beef tea or a beef extract such as Oxo.
The Menin Road ran straight through **The Salient** into **Jerry** lines,
and was littered with the remains of dead men and animals in shell
holes on every side. See also, **Cat meat**.

Mentioned in Despatches. Literally, to be mentioned by name in a
general's despatch to the War Office in London. It was a formal
recognition of good work, usually awarded to officers. In
conversation, it was abbreviated to 'a mention', or 'mensh'. The
name of the person so recognised was entitled to wear his mensh as
an oak leaf emblem on his campaign ribbons. See also, **Gazette**.

Mess. The place where soldiers ate. To mess down was to gather to eat.
Officers and **Other Ranks** ate separately, a peacetime distinction
that was strictly preserved on the **Western Front**. A mess president
administered the **mess fund** of the officers' mess, from which extra
luxuries were bought. A similar arrangement pertained in the
sergeants' mess. The job of a mess orderly was to fetch and serve
food. From Old French *mes*, dish of food.

Meteors. The Army's meteorologists. They were consulted most frequently by airmen but **staff** officers planning a gas attack also needed to keep an eye on wind speed and direction.

Methusilier. An old soldier. From a combination of **fusilier** and Methuselah, the oldest man in the Bible, reported to have lived for 969 years.

M.G., machine gun. The **Vickers** machine gun was mounted on a tripod and fired a belt of bullet cartridges fed in by hand. The **Lewis gun** was lighter and could be carried by one man. See also, **Emma gee**, **Mangle**.

Mick. An Irish soldier. The plural, Micks, covered any Irish regiment but specifically the Irish Guards. Mick was also the correct Army adjective for anything Irish. A mounted Mick was an Irish cavalryman, specifically a member of the 4th (Royal Irish) Dragoon Guards. See also, **Jock**.

Mick (2). The correct **lingo** for a pick, i.e. the heavy hand tool on a stave used in conjunction with the shovel for building and repairing **trenches**. From rhymimg slang. See also, **Banjo**.

Mills bomb. Tommy's favourite hand grenade. It was activated by a lever held in place by a pin. Invented by a Sunderland engineer, William Mills, the earliest version was issued in the spring of 1915. It was of little use in defence against a mobile **Jerry**, but it was very effective against him in **trenches**.

Mine. A large amount of explosive packed into a tunnel under an enemy position in order to blow it sky high. See also, **Sapper**.

Minge. The approved Army noun for womankind, the female sex in general.

Mingle. A social event at which soldiers and nurses could meet.

Minnie, Minniewopper, Moaning Minnie. A German **trench mortar**, *minenwerfer*, mine thrower, and its bomb. During daylight, a minnie could be seen in flight and therefore dodged. At night its imminent arrival was announced by a trail of sparks from its fuse. The explosion of this German **sausage** was so powerful it could kill by **concussion**.

Missing. A man was listed as missing if he was not present at **roll call** to answer his name and no one could say with certainty where he was. A man who was reported as missing in action was usually either lying dead and unburied or a prisoner of war. See also, **Red Cross Enquiry Office**.

Mister Sandbags. An airman's nickname for a dummy passenger. When a new pilot arrived at his **squadron** in France it was usual for him to be sent up on a test flight while his new comrades watched judgementally from the ground. If his plane was a two-seater, the weight of the **observer** would be simulated by loading the empty seat with sandbags.

M.M., Military Medal. A **gallantry** medal for **Other Ranks**, instituted in March 1916. **Old soldiers** regarded it as less prestigious than older awards which came with cash benefits. Also known as the **Machonachie** Medal.

M.O., Medical Officer. Every unit of any size had its own doctor, usually a volunteer serving as a **captain**. By the end of the war about half the doctors in Britain – some 22,000 men – had been taken into the Army. See also, **Number nine pill**.

Mob. A soldier's unit, his **company**, **battalion** or **brigade**, his home in the Army. From the Latin *mobile vulgus*, the fickle common folk.

Monkey meat. French corned beef. See also, **Bully**.

Moo-cow farm. Mouquet Farm. **Tommy**'s French. An infamous German fortress near the destroyed hamlet of Thiepval in the centre of the Somme battlefield.

Mop up, mop down. To absorb quantities of beer.

Mopping up. The process of winkling out the enemy after capturing his **trenches**, a job for bombers and **bayonet** men. See also, **Consolidation**.

Morgue, the. A nickname for the 3rd Division early in the war on account of its bad luck and high casualties. See also, **Signs**.

Morse code. The international alphabet for transmitting messages telegraphically. Morse could also be sent by wireless. See also, **Buzz**, **Iddy umpty**, **Signalese**.

Mother. All-purpose nickname for a British **heavy** gun but especially the 9.2 **how**. From its protective function. Also, mother was frequently reported to be the last word uttered by the dying. See also, **Grandma**.

Movies, the. Searchlights. They were used at night to illuminate **No Man's Land**. From the flickering black and white images of the first films.

Muck in, muckers. Muck in, to share. **Tommy**'s closest comrades were his **muckers**, those with whom he mucked in for food, drink, cigarettes and cash. Muckers looked out for each other's interests and pooled their resources.

Mudlarks. The Royal Engineers, the **sappers**. The phrase was also applied to any muddied person bursting into song.

Mufti. Civilian clothes. From the Hindustani *mufti*, a Muslim legal official allowed to wear his civilian clothes while on duty. See also, **Civvy**.

Mule train. See **Pack animal**.

Muscle in. To intrude greedily and without invitation on someone else's good fortune. An **N.C.O.**, for example, might use his seniority to muscle in on a group of **privates** sharing a food parcel or **brew** of hot **char**. See also, **Prat your frame in**.

Musical box. See **Whippet**.

Mustard. Keenness, aggression. See also, **Ginger up**.

Mustard gas. The most feared chemical weapon. First used by the Germans in July 1917. Unlike the other gases, which attacked men's breathing, mustard gas – dichlorethylsulphide – was a blistering agent, which attacked exposed skin. Gas masks were no protection. The oily liquid was extra dangerous because it could linger in shell holes until re-activated by the sun, at which point its fumes would rise again. See also, **Phosgene**.

Muzzle flash. The flare of gas produced by a gun when fired. Muzzle flash could give away the position of a gun, especially in dim light, so a flash cone might be fitted to hide the glare.

N

IS FOR

NUMBER
ON IT

Cross out anything below which does not apply.
Do not write anything on this side of the card except the date and your signature. If you write anything more than that, the card will be destroyed.

[Postage must be prepaid on any letter or post card addressed to the sender of this card.]

I am quite well.

I have been admitted into hospital

{ ~~sick~~ } and am going on well.
{ wounded } ~~and hope to be discharged soon.~~

I am being sent down to the base.

~~I have received your~~ { ~~letter dated~~ ....
{ ~~telegram dated~~ ....
{ ~~parcel dated~~ ....

Letter follows at first opportunity.

~~I have received no letter from you~~
{ ~~lately~~
{ ~~for a long time~~

SIGNATURE
ONLY } *Charles*

Date ....30/9/15....

Form A2042. 52914/701. 22Mm. P.Ltd. 2/44. 48/246.

Naik. The rank of corporal in the Indian Army. See also, Corp. **Sepoy**.

Name (on it). Every shell or bullet had a name or number on it. If it was your name, it would find you. See also, **Number up**.

'Napoleon's greeting to his troops!' A theatrical entertainment to relieve monotony in **trenches**. The man imitating Napoleon would announce his act with a fanfare and pose nobly with one hand tucked inside his tunic. Then, after a pause, he would fart or belch and say, 'Good morning, troops!' See also, **Gaff**.

Napoo. Gone, finished, no more. **Tommy**'s French. From *Il n'y en a plus*, there is no more. To napoo someone meant to kill him. Gone napoo meant dead. Napoo finee meant well and truly dead. See also, **'Good-bye-ee!'**, **'Mafeesh!'**, **Makoo**.

Navvying. Labouring with **banjo** and **mick** like the eighteenth-century navigators, navvies, who dug Britain's canal network. See also, **Digger**.

N.B.G. No Bloody Good.

N.C.O. Non-commissioned officer. His rank was indicated by the **stripes** on his sleeve. The officers of an **infantry battalion** exercised control through the agency of their N.C.O.s. If a **private** wanted to speak to an officer he had to do it by first approaching an N.C.O. See also, **Chevron**.

Neck, to get it in the. To be punished harshly. Also, to be badly wounded or killed.

Neighbours. Those in **field grey** on the other side of **No Man's Land**. Also, the vermin in one's own **trenches**, including rats. See also, **Chat**, **Livestock**.

New Army. See **Kitchener**.

'Nice day for it.' A sarcasm for bad weather, especially if it coincided with any undertaking likely to prove dangerous or unpleasant.

Nit. A hair louse. The prevalence of nits was one reason men kept their hair short. Also, derogatory for a **red cap**.

Nix. None, nil, nothing doing. **Tommy**'s German. From *nicht*, not.

'Nix goot.' No good. **Tommy**'s German. From *nicht gut*.

'No compree.' I don't understand. **Tommy**'s French. From *je n'ai pas compris*.

No Conscription Fellowship. An organisation set up after the introduction of the Derby scheme, in 1915, to oppose conscription and help **conchies** avoid it. See also, Conscript, Derby man.

No Man's Land. The area between the opposing **trench** lines, quiet by day, busier at night. The **staff** claimed No Man's Land as **Ours** but those who had to venture into it were often inclined to follow a live-and-let-live policy. The French sometimes used the word *billiard*, billiard table, for No Man's Land, a reminder that in summer, in quiet sectors, it became a green tangle of vegetation.

No treating. In June 1915 the government established a Control Board to regulate the distribution and sale of alcohol. In October that year it introduced a No Treating ban which forbade civilians from buying drinks for each other unless they were having a meal.

Nobody's Own. The 13th Hussars, the only cavalry **regiment** without royal or aristocratic patronage. See also, **God's Own**.

Non stop. A shell passing overhead. From the noise it made, like an express train rushing through a station without stopping.

Nose scratch. A bungled salute. See **Rookie**.

Nosebag. Literally, a feeding bag that fitted over a horse's head. Colloquially, a **gas hood**. As a verb, to nosebag meant to eat while on the move. If a piece of **gup** came straight from the nosebag of the colonel's horse it was deemed to be **jannack**.

'Not a sausage!' The complete absence of what was hoped for
– 'Mafeesh!'

'Not mit uns.' Not with us. **Tommy**'s German. A sarcasm derived from
the motto on **Jerry**'s belt clasp, *Gott mit uns*, God is with us.

Nous. Knowledge, cunning, shrewdness. From the Greek *nous*, mind.

'Now what?' The ritual question of troops arriving at their destination
to find no one to give them food, shelter or further orders. See also,
'Hurry up and wait!'

Number (on it). See **Regimental number**.

Number nine pill. The purgative routinely prescribed by the **M.O.** to
anyone who was not on the verge of death. Army medicine chests
were divided into numbered compartments, hence **No. 9** for the pills
kept in that compartment.

Number up. A premonition. 'My number's up' referred to the feeling
that pretty soon the speaker would be found by the bullet or shell
with his **number on it**. See also, **Name (on it)**.

Nut. The head. Also, a dandy, for which see **Knut**.

Nut it out. To work out the solution to a problem through brain power.

Nut worker. A schemer, a soldier given to **nutting it out**.

N.Y.D. Not Yet Diagnosed. A medical abbreviation. Sarcastically taken
to mean, Not Yet Dead. Other such abbreviations, daubed on the
casualty's forehead in blue pencil, included A.T. for any man
inoculated with anti-tetanus serum and M for anyone given
morphine.

IS FOR

OVER THE
BAGS

General Hospital 14,
British Expeditionary Force,
6th October, 1915.

Dearest M & F,

What a ghastly time you must have had. I am sorry not to have been able to write before. There was a certain amount of disorganisation after the battle, as you can imagine. It took days to get me down the line. You must have been worried sick when you got my _letter_ but the whole point of that was to assure you that although I had _copped one_ I was still in one piece. As for my wounds, there are two of them, both shrapnel balls. One hit my left shoulder and left a neat hole, the other smashed my right ankle and is still very painful. The _butchers_ have kept me back for another go at the foot but the shoulder seems to be healing quite nicely. So don't worry. I am coming home. I could be in _Blighty_ by the end of next week.

My overwhelming impression of the battle is one of great noise and confusion. To try to describe it would be pointless. All I can tell you for sure is that the order came to _go over_ at _zero_ and that the closer we got to _Jerry's_ line, the worse it got, although I was tremendously pleased with the way 'C' _Company_ performed in its first proper _show_. Some of my poor lads hardly got ten yards before

they were hit but my sergeant, Daniels, was a
tower of strength throughout, dodging the shell-
bursts and hustling men forward until we had
closed up with the firing line. There was no cover
whatsoever. Once the <u>Boche</u> got his guns onto us
we were simply pelted with <u>shrap.</u> According to
Welsh, a <u>sub</u> in 'D' Company who has fetched up
in this same <u>dock</u> with a <u>GSW</u> neck, our <u>casualties</u>
from beginning to end were about 330 men and
11 officers. They include Simmonds and Archie
Pratt from 'C', both dead, and Empson badly
wounded, all of them good Bridge players. The old doc
is heading this way so I will stop now and ask him
to get this off to you today rather than wait until
later.

  Much love,

  Charles

Observer. A junior officer assigned to watch **Jerry** from an **O.P.** A Forward Observation Officer, F.O.O., was an **artillery** observer sent up to locate targets and to correct the fall of shells around them. He was connected to his **guns** by a buzzer and had a **signaller** with him to keep the line intact. See also, **Buzz**, **Flying Arsehole**.

WILLS'S CIGARETTES.

A TRIBUTE TO THE R A M C.(FIELD AMBULANCE).

O.C., Officer Commanding. Not to be confused with **C.O., Commanding Officer.** When officers became **casualties**, the responsibility of command passed to survivors in line with seniority. Every unit needed an officer to command it therefore every officer was its potential O.C. By contrast, there was only one C.O., the man appointed by the Army to command that unit as his permanent job. Colloquially, O.C. was employed in various facetious applications. O.C. Donks, for example, was the Transport Officer, i.e. the officer commanding mules; O.C. Smokes was the officer who had just received a parcel of **fags**; O.C. Swills was in charge of **salvage**, etc., etc.

Off duty. A soldier's time to himself. Even when off duty he remained subject to military discipline. No soldier could wander about with his hands in his pockets or be seen improperly dressed. See also, **Knocking about**, **Rest**.

Off the map. A description for any place unknown or too far away to care about. Colloquially, to be 'off the map' was to be lost.

Officer Commanding. See **O.C.**

Official terms. If two officers disliked each other but had to work together for the sake of operations, they were said to be 'on official terms only'.

Oilskin. A trench coat impregnated with a water-repellent oil-based compound.

Old Bill. A cartoon character who became a British hero – an **Old Soldier** with a walrus moustache who was stoically resigned to being shelled out of his latest refuge as soon as he'd made it snug. He was created by an **infantry captain**, Bruce Bairnsfather, while in trenches south of **Eeps** in 1915.

Old China. A firm friend. See **China**.

Old Contemptible. A member of the original **B.E.F.**, which was purportedly described by the **Kaiser** in 1914 as a contemptibly small army.

Old Man. The **C.O.** of any unit. Compare the French *le Vieux*, the old man; the German *der Alte*, the old man.

Old soldier. At the start of the war, anyone in the **Regular Army** automatically became an old soldier. 'Don't come the old soldier with me' was a rebuke to any **Kitch** or **Derby man** presuming to know as much as his betters. Old soldiers were practised in **swinging the lead**, **dodging the column** and getting away with it. 'Old soldiers never die/ They simply fade away . . .'

Old Sweat. A regular who had served in garrisons around the Empire and especially in India. Hence the quantity of Hindustani in his **lingo**.

'On les aura!' A French war cry, 'We shall get them!' If not uttered as a sarcasm, it was likely to be answered with one. 'Get them yourself!'

On the nod. Any item acquired on the nod was free, gratis and probably stolen.

On the square. Drill. The square was the **parade** ground. Colloquially, someone described as being 'on the square' was deemed to be genuine or honest.

'On the word fix!' An **N.C.O.**'s warning phrase meaning, do it when I say so and not before. From the order for fixing **bayonets**: 'Fix bayonets . . . Fix!' The bayonet was not permitted to be clicked home until the final 'Fix!' was uttered.

'Once wounded, twice as windy.' A military version of the proverb 'Once bitten, twice shy.'

Onks. Francs. The French currency. See also, **Frong**.

Oofs. Eggs. **Tommy**'s French. From *oeufs*, eggs. If oofs didn't work, Tommy might try his Flemish, *eegs*. See also, **Erfs**.

Ooja-cum-pivvy. A gadget or **box of tricks**, any military thingama-jig.

Oojiboo. As above.

O.P., O.Pip. Observation post in **Signalese**, a place for watching the enemy in order to gather information about his movements. The O.P. might be in a **trench** or **sap** but wherever it was great care was taken to keep it secret. See also, **Observer**.

Open the bowling. To open the bowling was to be the first **mob** into the attack. From cricket. If the officers involved preferred dancing to wholesome sport they might prefer to speak of opening the ball.

WILLS'S CIGARETTES.

A TRIBUTE TO THE WOMEN WORKERS.

Opener. A laxative pill, for dealing with **conners**. See also, **Castor Oil Dragoons**.

Orchestra. The testicles. From rhyming slang. Orchestra stalls – balls. See also, **Goolies**.

Other Ranks. The enlisted, the non-commissioned, all **N.C.O.**s and **privates**, the men.

Ours. The widely used personal pronoun for anything British or **Allied**. The opposite of Ours was His or Theirs, anything belonging to **Jerry**. Hence the question of an **arrival**, 'Was that one of ours?'

'Over by Christmas.' An optimistic catchphrase from 1914 that became ironic thereafter, especially as the season of goodwill came round again each year.

Over the bags, Over the lid, Over the plonk, Over the top. To climb the **parapet** of one's **trench** and advance into **No Man's Land**.

IS FOR

POOR
BLOODY
INFANTRY

General Hospital 24,
British Expeditionary Force,
10ᵗʰ October, 1915.

Dear Edward,

I have given Ormond Square as my home
address to the medics in this new <u>dock</u> because I
want to be in London when they send me back to
<u>Blighty</u>. Unless things go drastically wrong that
should be some time in the next few days. I will
wire when I get the name of the hospital and the
date. Each time I think of it my heart skips a
beat. It reminds me of looking forward madly to
the long vac with just one, last, big house match to
win before the end of the season.

Do not believe anything you might have read
about our little scrap at Loos, it was a <u>lash-
up</u>. Our part in the proceedings was a minor
massacre, just one of several. The <u>Brigade</u>
objective was a fortified mill with its supporting
trench system. The scheme was to seize the mill,
then hold off <u>Jerry's</u> counter attacks for as long
as possible. Strategically, as I may have said
previously, the purpose was to pin him down to
prevent him interfering down south. Tactically,
it was a frontal attack behind a <u>creeping barrage.</u>
We had the <u>Jocks</u> on our left and the Indi-boys
on our right. While we watched our <u>gunners at</u>

work we saw through our field glasses that quite
a lot of Jerry's wire remained intact. The Old
Man was on the buzzer straight away but Brigade
simply repeated our orders – conform to the plan
as instructed. When the whistles blew we got a
grandstand view of the Jocks forming their line of
bayonets while a piper paraded on their parapet –
until a sniper got him. Everything seemed to be
going according to plan until our barrage started
to move. There was a deep drainage ditch running
across our front, almost bisecting No Man's Land.
When the first wave got there they found that their
bridging ladders were too short. It cost precious
minutes while the sappers scurried up and down
looking for bridgeheads. As the last of our smoke
screen blew off, Jerry's observers got their first
proper view and called up every gun they had.
By the time my lads got to the ditch it was a
bloody shambles, clogged with dead and wounded.
We were sitting ducks, not a stitch of cover in
sight. Simmonds tried to lead a charge, but too
late. Instead of staying on Jerry's line, to keep
him in his dug-outs, our barrage lifted forward
and left us with nowhere to hide. I saw Jocks and
Gurkhas tearing at the wire with their bare hands
but it was as thick as a hedge and six feet high in
places. Jerry's shrapnel flayed us alive. Then,
when the Hun got his emma gees onto his parapet
as well – he simply hosed us off the field. The burst

that hit me tipped me sideways towards a shell hole
and someone must have pulled me in but I don't
remember it. I crawled back that night on one knee
and one elbow, through a field of corpses. Some
of those poor Jocks were still twitching, sprawled
in the mud with their kilts all awry and their bare
arses gleaming in the moonlight.

It was not glorious, Edward. It was murder. It
was a <u>lash-up</u> from start to finish. It was sheer
bloody murder. There's no point denying it. The
only, meagre, consolation is that somehow I have
come out of it in one piece. So far I have never
had cause to doubt that we have the beating of
these Jerries but not if we carry on like this. As
an example of <u>staff</u> work it was embarrassingly
amateur. We paid for it in the slaughter of fine
men. It makes me feel sick to the pit of my
stomach.

I'd better stop. I could go on like this for page
after page but I think I've said enough.

Yours ever,

Charles

Pack animal. A horse or **donk** for carrying loads in **panniers** or a special pack saddle. A **mule train** was a string of pack animals and their attendants. The verb to pack meant to transport material by mule train or, if mules were not available, by **infantry**.

Packet. A wound. To cop a packet was to get wounded.

Padre. A military chaplain, a minister of religion in uniform, a pulpit **wallah**. From the Spanish *padre*, father, a Roman Catholic priest. The most famous padre in the Army was an Anglican, Geoffrey Studdert Kennedy, known as **Woodbine Willie**. See also, **Devil dodger**.

'Pain in his little finger.' A malady ascribed to any **malingerer** or hypochondriac.

Paint. Jam.

Pals. Volunteers who joined the **infantry** in 1914–15 on the understanding that they would serve together in the same **battalions**, e.g. Bradford Pals, Salford Pals. The great test of the pals' battalions of **Kitchener's Army** was the Battle of the Somme, 1916.

Pannier, pan. A basket or canvas carrier used for transporting gear on **donks**. Also, the name for a **drum** of ammunition for the **Lewis gun**.

Parabellum. The jargon name of a type of semi-automatic **Jerry** pistol and machine gun. From the Latin *si vis pacem, para bellum*, if you seek peace prepare for war.

Parade. Any ordered gathering of soldiers for **drill**, instruction or **issue** of **rations**.

Parados. Earth piled along the back of the **trench**. Without a parados, the head of any man popping up to look over the **parapet** might reveal him against the skyline, thereby offering a target.

Parapet. Excavated earth banked along the front of a **trench**. If it was a **fire trench** the parapet might well be strengthened with sandbags and steel plates fitted with loopholes.

Paris gun. A giant German gun for bombarding Paris. Its tube was so long (128 feet) it shook like a fishing rod when fired. The first one was used on 23 March 1918, hurling its shell an unheard of distance of 75 miles. In all, 256 people were killed by these monsters.

Park. A place for keeping military vehicles or equipment, hence lorry park, gun park. **Tanks**, however, were parked in a tankodrome, where their fronts were draped in sheets called horn covers to disguise their distinctive shape from prying **Jerry** aircraft.

Parole. The word of honour of an officer. The promise given by a prisoner of war.

Part worn. The correct Army adjective for second-hand clothing or kit, as **salvaged** from the dead or wounded and re-issued. Part-worn items could often be bartered for something better if a little **bunce** was added.

Pass. The authorisation necessary to leave camp or **billets**. Without a pass a soldier was likely to be judged out of bounds, which was a **crime**.

Pass out. Passing out was the **parade** that marked the end of a course of instruction. Colloquially, to pass out meant to die.

Pass muster. To pass muster was to reach the required standard at an inspection or to perform without rebuke on **parade**. From the Latin *monstrare*, to point out, to show.

Patrol. A foray into **No Man's Land** to check on the enemy or seize prisoners.

Pay book. The Army book issued to each soldier for recording his pay and promotions. It also served as his identity document, containing his name, **regiment** and **regimental number**. At the back was a page for a 'will', which included the address of the next of kin. The pay book was carried at all times, in the tunic breast pocket.

P.B.I., Poor Bloody Infantry. The phrase for foot soldiers used by the rest of the Army and applied to the **infantry** by themselves with a mixture of defiance and self-pity. Infantry derives from Spanish, the kings of Spain being the first European monarchs to raise **regiments** of full-time professional troops. The Spanish princes were called *Infantas*, children of the royal house. When the *Infantas* were attached in an honorary capacity to their fathers' regiments they became known as *Infanteria*.

P.D.Q. Pretty Damn Quick.

Pea shooter. Rifle.

Peace offensive. A sarcastic phrase for any overture from the enemy to talk peace.

Peaceful penetration. A tactic developed later in the war for attacking the enemy with tanks, artillery and aircraft simultaneously, an early form of what later became known as *blitzkrieg*. The aim was to drive the enemy from his **trenches** by firepower so they could be penetrated without heavy casualties to the **P.B.I.**

Pear drops. Tear gas, from its sweet and sickly smell. See also, **Gas alert**.

Pediculi. A Latinism for vermin. An officers' jocularity. *Pediculus capitis* was the head louse, the **nit**. *Pediculus vestimenti* was the body louse. *Pulex irritans* was the flea.

Peechy, peechi. Presently, in a short while. "Alf a mo', I'll be there peechy.'

Pen pusher. A clerk, an office worker. See also, **Ink slinger**.

Penguin. A member of the Women's Section of the Royal Air Force, a W.R.A.F. From the flight-less nature of the penguin. W.R.A.F.s were allowed to drive cars but not fly aircraft.

Perisher. Trench periscope. See also, **Looking stick**.

'Permission to speak, sir!' The formula required before one of the **Other Ranks** could address an officer without having been addressed by him first.

Persuader. Bayonet.

Petrol can. A two-gallon container for carrying drinking water to the **trenches**. The insides of used petrol cans were meant to be seared with flame to prevent contamination but most water reaching the front line in petrol cans did indeed taste of petrol.

P-helmet. A **gas hood** with eye pieces, introduced during 1915.

Phosgene. The deadliest and most feared of **Jerry**'s war gases, introduced in 1917. He called it *Lost*; **Tommy** called it **mustard gas**, from its yellowish colour and slightly mustard smell. See also, **Yellow cross**.

Phyllis. Euphemism for syphilis. Later in the war, venereal disease was categorised as a **self-inflicted wound** and **Other Ranks** would have their pay stopped for the duration of their treatment, an imposition not levied on officers. See also, **Wasserman test**.

Pi jaw. Pious talk, uplifting words, perhaps from a **padre**.

Piccadilly Cowboys. See **Household Cavalry**.

Pick off. To watch a target and destroy it with careful aim. See also, **Sniper**.

Picket. A sentry posted in front of his **battalion**'s line. On the **Western Front** this put him somewhere out in **No Man's Land**, probably in a shell hole or **sap**.

Pickford's Light Horse. Civilian lorries pressed into military service with the **A.S.C.** in 1914. Apart from the hundreds of London buses sent to France, a mixed fleet of delivery vans was also commandeered, all in their commercial livery. Pickford's was a haulage and removal firm with depots across Britain. See **Ally Sloper's Cavalry**.

Pickled monkey. Any unidentifiable meat.

Picnic, picnic spot. Sarcastic phrase for a dangerous part of the **Line**.

Piece. Woman. Also, a **gun**. See also, **Bint**, **Red Lamp**.

Piece of Paper. The Treaty of London, signed in 1839, by which the European powers, including Germany, agreed to respect Belgian neutrality. **Jerry**'s violation of this treaty led to Britain's Declaration of War, 4 August 1914.

Pig's ear. Beer. Rhyming slang.

Pill. A bomb, dropped from an aircraft. See also, **Egg**.

Pill box. A concrete fortlet with room for at least one machine gun.

Pimple. Any small but definite eminence of terrain. In **trench nomenclature**, pimple became a synonym for hill.

Pinard. Rough wine issued daily to French troops.

Pineapple. A type of **trench mortar** bomb.

Pink, in the. A formulaic valediction or greeting in British letters home. 'Hoping this finds you as it leaves me, still in the pink and thinking of you all . . .' From racing jargon, a horse in fine fettle being described as in the pink of condition.

Pioneer. A military labourer. From the Old French *pionnier*, foot soldier. Each British **division** had a **battalion** of pioneers for heavy manual work, not for combat, although they all carried rifles. 'God made the bee/ The bee made honey/ Pioneers do the work/ The **sappers** get the money.'

Piou-Piou. The French equivalent of **Tommy** at the start of the war, the nickname of the representative **private**. See also, **Poilu**.

Pip. A stud of cloth or brass worn on the sleeve or shoulder strap to indicate an officer's rank. One pip, second lieutenant; two pips, **lieutenant**; three pips, **captain**. The phrase 'one pip, one **stunt**' suggests how promotion was earned.

Pipe opener. A short, sharp exertion sufficient to open the breathing pipes, i.e. lungs. Colloquially, the first **fag** of the day.

WILLS'S CIGARETTES.

A TRIBUTE TO THE ANZACS

Pipsqueak. A rifle grenade. Also derogatory for a field gun or its shell, a **whizz-bang**. Colloquially, any shortish, impertinent comrade.

Pish. Scotch whisky. An esteemed officers' restorative.

'Pity the poor sailor on a night like this.' An ironic acknowledgement of foul weather from men in a flooded **trench**.

Plaster. To inflict a heavy bombardment on a particular area. The German equivalent was *beplastern*. To get plastered was to get drunk.

Platoon. One of four sub-units of an **infantry company**. A platoon was commanded by a second lieutenant, with a **sergeant** to assist. Each platoon had four sections of 16 men (nominally) each under a **corporal** or **lance jack**. From French, **peloton**, a knot or string of men. The cavalry equivalent of a platoon was a **troop**.

Plinkity plonk. White wine. **Tommy**'s French. From *vin blanc*, white wine. Red wine was never a favourite. Champagne, when obtainable, was guzzled by all.

Plonk. Wine. See above. Also, mud. Also, the **Ditch** or **Pond**.

Plug. A chunk of tobacco, given as **issue** to pipe smokers instead of **fags**. It could also be chewed. As a verb, to plug someone was to shoot him, plug him with lead, except among **poultice wallopers**, for whom plug meant a wad of lint to staunch a wound.

Plug away. To show dogged persistence in harrying the enemy. A determination to plug away at it was essential in a war of **attrition**.

Plum and apple. The ubiquitous flavour of **issue** jam. Strawberry or raspberry rarely got further than the **quartermaster**. Jam came in tins not jars. See also, **Paint**, **Pozzie**, **Tickler**.

Po juggler. An officer's **batman**, po being the short form of chamber pot.

Poilu. The French infantry **private**. Literally, the hairy one. It took over from **piou-piou** when the French newspapers got a firmer grip on what infantry actually looked like after a tour of duty in the **trenches**. As with **Tommy**, *poilu* was more popular with officers and **ink slingers** than the **Other Ranks**.

Point blank. White wine. From the French *blanc*, white. See also, **Plinkity plonk**.

Point blank range. Literally, the range at which no soldier could miss the target. French derivation. The centre of the target – the equivalent of the English bullseye – was white in France, *point blanc*.

Pond. The Atlantic Ocean or English Channel. See also, **Ditch**, **Drink**.

Poodle faker. A smarmy, well-groomed type interested rather too much in **minge**.

Pop. Poperinghe, a fabled **joy spot** behind **The Salient**.

Pop the parapet, pop the bags. See **Over the top**.

Pop wallah. A teetotaller. From pop, any fizzy soft drink.

Postal order. A money voucher which could be bought at one Post Office and redeemed at any other for its full cash value. During the war, postal orders were the surest and most convenient way of getting pounds, shillings and pence to and from the **trenches**.

Pot. To shoot hopefully. Hence potting and pot shot.

Potato masher. The main **Jerry** hand grenade. The **box of tricks** was screwed onto a wooden handle, hence also the names stick grenade and truncheon. It could be thrown further than the Mills bomb but it was less lethal in its effects.

Potted dog. Tinned meat. See also, **Bully beef**, **Pickled monkey**.

Poultice walloper. A medical person. See also, **Linseed Lancers**.

Pox. Venereal disease. See also, **Clap**, **Phyllis**.

Pow wow. A conference of officers, especially **brass hats**.

Pozzie. Jam.

Prat your frame in. To intrude without invitation. 'Oi! This is a private game. Who asked you to prat your frame in?' See also, **Muckers**.

Primus. A portable cooker fuelled by a canister of paraffin which was pumped through a gas ring to give a strong blue flame. The Primus did not give off smoke, which meant it could be used in even the most forward positions.

Princess Mary's gift. A present to the armed forces from the royal family at Christmas, 1914. A public appeal raised more than £130,000 to send soldiers and sailors a brass box containing a greetings card, **fags** and chocolate.

Private. The lowest rank in the Army. From private sentinel, a soldier holding no rank. A private in a fusilier regiment was a **fusilier**; a private in a rifle regiment was a rifleman; a private in a **Guards** regiment was a **guardsman**; a private in the Artillery was a **gunner**; a private in the Royal Engineers was a **sapper**; a private in the cavalry was a **trooper**; one name covered them all, **Tommy**.

'Promenade, Mamzel? Prom'nay?' Tommy's French. His invitation to a mademoiselle to take a walk, with the aim of **clicking** with her.

WILLS'S CIGARETTES

Prophylaxis. A jargon word used by **poultice wallopers** to refer to the inoculation of troops against disease. See also, **Jab**.

Proto man. A soldier equipped with breathing apparatus in order to enter a deep mine full of poisonous gas (usually carbon monoxide). From the firm that made it, Proto. The breathing kit consisted of goggles and breathing tubes connected to a heavy pouch of chemicals worn on the chest. See also, **Canary**.

Prussian Guard. A flea or **chat**. See also, **Welsh cricket**.

P.T. Physical Training. See **Jerk**.

P.T.I. Physical Training Instructor. See also, **Basher**, **Canary**.

Pudding basin. The British steel helmet. See also, **Battle bowler**, **Tin lid**.

Pukka. Real, authentic. From the Hindustani *pakha*, cooked, ripe. In a battalion of **Kitcheners** there might be a leavening of regular officers and **N.C.O.**s who would regard themselves as the pukka soldiers. The opposite of pukka was cutcha, unripe.

Pung. To fall asleep while on buzzer work. **Signallers'** colloquial. See also, **Buzz**.

Push. A large-scale offensive involving several **divisions**. A push was delivered in several stages and sustained over a period of weeks or months. To give someone or something the push was to arrange for his or its abrupt departure.

Put in. Staff officers' jargon. They did not send troops into battle, they put them in.

Puttee. The **khaki** binding from ankle to knee when a soldier was in uniform. From the Hindustani *patti*, bandage.

Putty medal. A common and therefore disparaged **gong**, given out wholesale by a grateful British nation or its **Allies**. The French *Croix de Guerre* was particularly widespread. Other such foreign awards included the Egyptian Order of the Nile, the Portuguese Order of Aviz, the Russian Order of St Anne, the Greek Order of the Redeemer and the Serbian Order of St Sava.

Pyjama sector. A quiet stretch of the line where the **billets** were so safe officers felt able to wear their pyjamas in bed. See, **Armin**.

IS FOR

QUEER

6th West Kent Fusiliers,
British Expeditionary Force,
26th March, 1916.

Dear Edward,

I am back in the war again and feeling pretty sick
with life. At Southampton I was given a draft of
rookies to bring over and it almost broke my heart.
They were <u>keen as mustard</u> for their chance to give
<u>Jerry</u> a whack but painfully unready for what it
will cost them. The hillsides are covered with endless
camps and <u>hutments.</u> We <u>P.B.I.</u> have become mere
military manpower, to be sorted according to type for
the mincing machine. My temper is not improved by
the refusal of my smashed foot to heal properly. Nor
does it help lift my spirits that along with my extra
<u>pip</u> has come a transfer to the Sixth Battalion (note
new address above) which was sprung on me entirely
without warning. I feel sick about that, too. Still,
tonight's <u>billet</u> is a <u>cushy</u> one. I am in the Officer's
Club and do not <u>go up</u> until tomorrow or the day after.
There's the dinner gong. Will resume later . . .

(27th March) Forgive the somewhat inelegant hand.
I am feeling decidedly <u>queer</u> and have reported sick
to get over it. On my way into dinner last night I
bumped into Rodney Marshall, one of the regulars I
<u>mucked in</u> with back in the Hazeley Down days. He
is a <u>captain</u> now, on his way back to <u>Division</u> covered

in <u>red tabs</u> after completing his <u>staff</u> course. Once I had finished telling him about Loos and my wounds, etcetera, he offered to try to <u>wangle</u> me a temporary billet as a staff learner, since he is well in with his general.

Rodders has been here three days already and is quite the Master of Ceremonies. After coffee, he sat me down for my first lesson in staffwork. He ordered up three bottles of fizz and bid me pay close attention. First, he tapped the top of the table with one finger, both hands, then he tapped the underside of the table with one finger, both hands, then he snapped his fingers once, both hands, and picked up his drink between one finger and thumb, tapped the table with it and knocked it back. Then it was my turn. Rodders was deady serious. If I had got one tap or sip in the wrong order I would have failed the test and he wouldn't have taken me. Then it was everyone else's turn. If one of us made a mistake he had to drain his glass and re-charge and start again. And so it went until the shampoo ran out and we switched to brandy and then, one by one, slipped off our chairs. It is a funny war, this war. I am not sure I like it as much as before.

Yours as ever,

Charles

Q.M., Quartermaster, Quarter-bloke. Every Army unit had a
Quartermaster whose job was to manage the supply of **rations** and
kit, including uniforms. He was responsible for the quantity of food
and drink but not its quality. The Q.M. of an **infantry battalion** was
normally a **ranker**, an **N.C.O.** promoted to be an officer, usually a
lieutenant. As such, he was meant to be wise to the wiles of **Old
Sweats**.

Q.M.S. A quartermaster sergeant, an **N.C.O.** appointed to assist
the **Q.M.**

Quaker. A member of the Christian
sect, the Society of Friends.
Colloquially, a conscientious
objector. Some Quakers went to
jail for refusing conscription,
others served as medical orderlies
in France. See also, **Conchie**
Conscript.

Quarter. To give quarter was to
show mercy to a wounded or
captured enemy.

Queer. Unwell, indisposed.

Qui vive. On the alert. If a soldier
was on the _qui vive_ he was under
orders to be extra vigilant. French
derivation, from the **sentry**'s
challenge, 'Who lives?'

Quick Dick. An artillery piece fitted with a recoil system that enabled
it to fire shells in quick succession. The German quick-firer, the
Krupp 77 mm, could manage a comfortable 5 shells per minute. The
French Soixante Quinze banged away at 15 **rounds** per minute. The
British 18-pounder, manned by a nimble detachment, might be able

to fire as many as 20 rounds per minute. See also, **Whizz-bang**.

Quick squirt. A short **burst** of fire from an **emma gee**. See also, **Hose**.

Quill driver. A soldier employed as a clerk. See also, **Ink slinger**.

Quillion. The curved hook between handle and blade on a **bayonet**, a useful feature for holding candles in **trench** or **dug-out**, hence **candlestick**.

Quimp. An Army adjective meaning sloppy or unmilitary in demeanour.

R

IS FOR

RED TAB

HQ, 198th Infantry <u>Brigade</u>,
British Expeditionary Force,
1st April, 1916.

Dear Mudge and Fudge,

No doubt you have already heard from Teddy
about my sudden but strictly temporary elevation
to the dizzying heights. I must say, a pair of
scarlet tabs on the collar does give one a different
way of looking at life. Whenever things went
wrong in <u>The Salient</u> last year, we <u>P.B.I.</u> always
assumed that some over-promoted fool of a <u>brass</u>
<u>hat</u> had made a hash of his job. The plain fact is,
the Army out here is expanding every day and
running it is becoming ever more complicated.
Hence the need for clever young chaps like
me. Never forget that the <u>Hun</u> has all the best
positions and is very stoutly dug in. He has no
intention of giving up a single inch of what he's
won. To shift him we need to be not only better
than he is but bigger, which means bigger guns
and more men. More men require more <u>fodder</u> and
kit. More fodder and kit requires more lorries. More
lorries require more roads. Etcetera, etcetera. Nor
should you imagine, just because I am now living
in a chateau, that our way of life is luxurious.
Our general can be quite jolly in the <u>mess</u> but he
is an absolute stickler when it comes to work. He

is up at six every morning and expects the rest of
us to be up then too. Sometimes I manage a ride
before breakfast but there are not enough nags to
go round so usually it is straight down to brekker
and from there straight to the desk. All those
men and rations require an inordinate quantity
of _signals, chits_ and _idents_ to speed them up the
line. So far I am enjoying it, but I do miss the old
batt and the lads of 'C' _Coy_ and their _backchat_. Our
general expects us to laugh uproariously at his
jokes but he is not so keen on sharing the limelight.

Hope this finds you _in the pink_ as ever,
your loving son,

Charles (Apprentice General) . . .

Rafale. The term for successive intense periods of shelling intended to paralyse and confuse. From the French *rafale*, a sudden gust of bad weather.

Ragtime. A disparaging adjective for slackness and all-round inferiority. Derived from the loosely syncopated jazz music arriving in **Blighty** with the **Yanks**.

Railhead. The closest place to the **Front** reached by standard gauge railway. **Staff** jargon. A railhead was where stores or men had to be de-trained in order to complete the journey by road.

Railway Transport Officer, R.T.O. Every railway station of any size on the **Western Front** had an Army R.T.O. attached. It was to him that **infantry** in transit turned for information about food, drink and the whereabouts of the next train. Any man who missed his train had to get the R.T.O. to stamp or sign his **chit**, his travel warrant in order to secure **rations** and accommodation. By missing trains, or catching the wrong train accidentally on purpose, a soldier could take days making his way back up the **Line** after a spell of **leaf** or attending a course at the **base**.

R.A.M.C., Royal Army Medical Corps. See **Castor Oil Dragoons**.

Rank out. To rank someone out was to expel him from a desirable **billet** or **dug-out** by authority of superior rank.

Ranker. An **N.C.O.** promoted from the ranks to be an officer. Only one soldier by 1918 had risen from the lowest to the highest rank – Field Marshal Sir William Robertson, Chief of the Imperial General Staff, nicknamed **Wullie**, who started his career as a trooper.

Rapatry. A **Frog** or **Belgie** expelled from occupied German territory in order to reduce the number of women, children and old men **Jerry** had to feed. Able-bodied men were kept as forced labour. From the French *repatrie*, one repatriated.

Rat. To steal from a corpse. Also, to relieve a **Jerry** prisoner of **souvenirs**.

Rations. Food destined for the **trenches** was either dry or wet. Dry rations comprised **hard tack** or soft, and anything in a tin. Wet rations comprised **burgoo**, **char**, **skilly** and any cooked food delivered in a **dixie**.

R.E. The Royal Engineers, known throughout the Army as **sappers** from their historic function, the undermining (sapping) of enemy fortifications.

Reading your shirt. To look for lice in the seams of one's **greyback** See also, **Chat**.

Rear-up. A noisy quarrel that might lead to a stand up, a proper fight with fists.

Recce. To reconnoitre, to locate the enemy and report back.

Red caps. Military police. From the red cover worn over their caps. Red caps were despised by the **Other Ranks** because it was thought their jobs kept them out of serious danger.

Red Cross Enquiry Office. The British Red Cross ran a bureau in London to help relatives trace **casualties** posted as **missing**. Red Cross volunteers would track down a missing man's comrades and interview them, if possible, to find out what had happened. They also kept up-to-date lists of prisoners of war.

Red Hussar. A brand of **fag** made for the Army and distributed as **issue**.

Red ink. Red wine.

Red Lamp. A brothel for **Other Ranks**. Officers' brothels were advertised by a blue lamp. The French euphemism for brothel was *maison tolerée*, a permitted house. See **Blue Lamp**.

Red tab. A **staff** officer. From his scarlet collar tab. Known by some as the Red Badge Of Funk. See also, **Gorget**.

Refused flank. See **Flank**.

Regiment. The parent organisation of an **infantry battalion**. Before the war the normal number of full-time battalions in a British regiment was two, one of which was nearly always overseas, usually in India. During the war, as volunteers and **conscripts** poured in, a regiment became a machine for replicating itself, battalion by battalion.

Regimental. A career officer or **N.C.O.** of strong loyalty to his **regiment** with no driving ambition to be promoted out of it. A regimental might be inclined to be suspicious of **staff** officers. Regimental was also the adjective for anyone deemed to be excessively strict in matters pertaining to precedence and military good form. As far as uniform was concerned, regimentals referred to the full dress uniform worn by a regiment on ceremonial occasions, as opposed to the **khaki** worn on active service.

Regimental number. Every soldier was given a number when he enlisted. It was written in his **pay book** and became part of his identity. At **roll call**, regimental numbers were used to distinguish between any two men of the same surname. If a man won a **gong**, his number as well as his name was punched into its rim.

Regimental Sergeant Major, R.S.M. The senior **N.C.O.** in an **infantry battalion**, the regimental for short. He was likely to be a physically imposing specimen with a strong word of command and a considerable fund of **language**.

Regular Army. The standing army of Great Britain. In 1914 it consisted of about 125,000 full-time officers and men, professional soldiers who had joined the Army as a career. By comparison, France had a standing army of 700,000, with 4.2 million in reserve. Germany kept 840,000 men in uniform, with 5 million in reserve. See also, **Terrier**.

Relief. A soldier charged with taking over a duty from another. In the **Line**, **sentries** relieved sentries, **companies** relieved companies, **battalions** relieved battalions. A typical rotation of battalions within a **brigade** might be: four days in the front line; four days in support; four days in reserve; four days' rest. The unit coming into the line to relieve the one on duty was known as the relief. In a well-conducted relief, officers would be shown around and given an accurate **ident** of **trench stores**. Most reliefs took place at night. They were meant to be conducted quickly and silently for fear of alerting the enemy. See also, **Last lot in**.

'Remember Belgium.' Originally a recruiting slogan, this phrase was later invoked sarcastically by those mired in **The Salient**.

Remount. A fresh horse or **donk** to replace one wounded or killed. They were gathered in at remount **depots** in **Blighty** before being shipped to France. Apart from the cavalry and artillery requirements, each **infantry battalion** was supposed to have 62 horses for its transport needs. At one point the British Army was feeding 600,000 horses and 200,000 mules per day. Colloquially, remount was a disparagement of a particular type of woman.

Renault. A French-built light tank, comparable in design to the British **Whippet** but slower.

Reserved occupation. A civilian job of such importance to the war effort that anyone doing it was exempt from conscription when the first Military Service Act was introduced in 1916. At one point there were 160 jobs on the list. Coal-miners and men working in munitions factories and ship-building were all safe. See also, Conscript.

Resipator. Facetious term for a gas mask.

Respirator. The correct jargon for a gas mask. It was also applied to other lifesaving innovations. The cork waistcoats issued to men on cross-Channel boats were also sarcastically called respirators.

Rest. Any period spent out of the **Line**. For fighting troops, rest meant working parties, **fatigues**, field exercises, **footslogging** and **drill**.

Rest camp. Cemetery. See also, **Stiff's paddock**.

Revally, Reveille. Waking-up time, pronounced re-valley. From the French **revailler**, to wake up. In the French army, the wake-up call was known as the *diane*.

Rhino. Money. Also, cheese.

Rifle grenade. A grenade with a metal rod attached that enabled it to be fired from a rifle. The rod went into the barrel of the rifle and a blank cartridge was used to shoot it in the direction of **Jerry**'s **trenches**. Rifle grenades were not fired with the rifle held against the shoulder but with its butt placed on the ground so it could be fired in the style of a mortar.

Right of the Line. See **Royal Horse Artillery**.

Ring money. The Army separation allowance deducted from a man's pay for the upkeep of his family in **Blighty**. Derived from wedding ring, the seal of marriage.

'Rise and shine!' The orderly **corporal**'s morning greeting to his men. 'Rise and shine! Hands off your cocks! Put on your socks!'

Rissole King. A **babbler**. From rissole, an offal and onion meatball cooked in gravy more commonly known as an arsehole. See also, **'Who called the cook a bastard?'**

R.N.D., Royal Naval Division. An Army **division** formed by sailors who, at the start of the war, were found to be surplus to the Royal Navy's requirements. They were turned into soldiers at the urging of Winston Churchill. Each **battalion** in the R.N.D. was named after a famous admiral. It became the Army's 63rd Division in 1916 but persisted in its naval traditions. Its men did not go on **leaf**, they went ashore and they called their cookhouse a galley.

R.O.D. See **Duration**.

Roger. Code word for a cylinder of poison gas and a nickname for rum. Also, as a verb, to have sex with someone. The rare indulgence in rum and sex at the same time might be described as a right royal rogering.

Roll call. The **parade** at which each man affirmed his continued presence. In **trenches**, the **corporal** of any section would perform this duty and report to the **sergeant**, who would report to the **platoon** commander, who would report to the **company** commander, who would report to the **adjutant**. See also, **Missing**.

WILLS'S CIGARETTES.

A TRIBUTE TO CANADA

Roman candle. A Roman Catholic. See also, **C of E, Follow the band**.

Rookie, rooky. A recruit. See also, **Tyro**.

Rooti, rooty. Bread. From the Hindustani *roti*, bread. At the start of the war the Army ration was one two-pound loaf between four men. See also, **Japan**.

Rooti medal. A Long Service medal, the implication being that it had been earned by sitting around for years eating **rations**.

Rosalie. The French infantry **bayonet**. Unlike the British **sword**, Rosalie was a spike. Also known as *la forchette*, the fork, *tire-bouchon*, the corkscrew and *coupe-choux*, the cabbage knife. Rosalie was the patron saint of the French town of Bayonne, whence the bayonet was said to have originated.

Round. A single bullet or shell was called a round. Historic jargon. From the days when muskets and cannon fired round balls of lead.

Route march. A training **drill** inflicted during **rest**. Men would be marched for between 10 and 20 miles, depending on their loads. In the Army, route was pronounced rout.

Royal Artillery. The biggest regiment in the British Army. **Privates** in the Royal Artillery were called **gunners**, **corporals** were bombardiers. The Royal Artillery has no flag, its guns are its colours; they are saluted on **parade**.

Royal Flying Corps, R.F.C. The part of the **Regular Army**, which in 1914 consisted of less than a thousand men of all ranks, whose job was experimenting with the military applications of aeroplanes. The R.F.C. started the war with three **squadrons**, comprising 63 planes, most of which went to France in crates. By the time the war ended, there were 99 squadrons in France and the Royal Air Force consisted of more than 50,000 men.

Royal Horse Artillery, R.H.A. The **artillery** arm of the cavalry. When on parade with its guns, the R.H.A. takes precedence over every regiment in the Army, **Right of the Line**.

Ruddy. Euphemism for the swear word **bloody**. When George Bernard Shaw put bloody into the mouth of Eliza Doolittle in *Pygmalion*, at its London premiere, 11 April 1914, the scandal was such that one London newspaper, the *Sketch*, implored him to change it to ruddy.

Ruhleben. An internment camp for **Allied** civilians at the main Berlin race track. Some 4,000 British tourists and businessmen were stranded in Germany or Belgium at the beginning of the war and spent the whole four years at Ruhleben.

Ruin. Tommy's French for Rouen.

Rum. See **S.R.D.**

Rum train. The **fatigue** party sent under escort, to collect the rum ration and distribute it, without diminution, to its intended recipients. See **S.R.D.**

Runner. A military messenger. Every unit needed runners to get messages through in the event of signal wires being cut by bombardment. See also, **Galloper**.

IS FOR

SOUVENIR

HQ, 198th Infantry Brigade,
British Expeditionary Force,
8th April, 1916.

Dearest Mudge,

I hope the enclosed battlefield memento will raise
a smile. The detail is quite charming. I found it
yesterday in a town which reminded me of Queen
Victoria's favourite husband. It was the first time
I have been able to have a good poke around on my
own. The town is not a complete shambles, it is
too important for that. Sappers hide in the cellars
and keep the main roads clear for transport and
troops. However, for one moment I did feel like a
proper tourist — standing directly under the Golden
Virgin, gaping up at her, wondering if she was
going to fall on me freakishly and thereby secure
me an unheroic footnote when the history of this
war comes to be written. Jerry's gunners take pot
shots at it every now and then but they are too far
away to get a good go at her and unlikely to get any
closer in the near future.

What was once an obscure provincial town is
now a collection of ruins. The sense of desolation
is most affecting. There is hardly a house intact.
Most of the rooves have been blown into the
gardens. Among the heaped wreckage of some
family's wildly overgrown lawn I sat in a patch

of sunlight to absorb the melancholy. Two thrushes busied themselves with this year's nest. The war must end sometime. One spring day the <u>Frogs</u> will return to put their rooves back on and weed their cabbages again but it will be many years before their town looks human again. Sometimes, Mudge, I feel as if I am taking part in a crime rather than a crusade.

God help us all and Happy Easter.
Your loving, living, doubting son,

Charles

Salient. Any part of a **trench** line bulging into enemy territory. Salients were vulnerable to **enfilade fire** and therefore costly to defend.

Salient, The. On the **Western Front** the use of the definite article, **The Salient**, referred to the bulge in the line around **Eeps**, our defence of which barred **Jerry**'s route to the Channel ports and the main supply lines of the **B.E.F.**

Salvage. Discarded or damaged items of uniform or equipment. After a battle, anything that could be re-used was meant to be collected at the salvage dump, from where it was taken down to the **base** to be cleaned, refurbished and re-issued. Used brass shell cases and cartridge cases were salvaged in their millions. From the Latin root *salvus*, safe. See also, **Part worn**.

WILLS'S CIGARETTES.

A TRIBUTE TO SOUTH AFRICA

Salvo. All the guns of an **artillery** battery firing at once. From the Spanish *salva*, a taste of something, a salutation.

Sam Brown. The British officer's brown leather harness, a strap coming up from the back of the belt, over the right shoulder and fastening at the front by the left hip. Named after its inventor, a **V.C.** winner who lost his left arm in the Indian Mutiny. Some discarded the Sam Brown in action as it attracted the attention of **Jerry** snipers; others thought that was a very good reason for keeping it on.

'San fairy Ann!' Forget it! Never mind! *Tommy*'s French. From *ça ne fait rien*, that doesn't matter. To describe someone as san-fairy-annie implied laziness or thoughtlessness. The phrase was also used as a fatalistic reply to any warning or caution. 'It's all san-fairy-ann to me, mate. If it happens it happens . . .'

Sanitary squad. Men assigned to the digging of **latrines**, emptying of buckets and the disinfecting with **chloride of lime** of those places where bodies had been improperly or hurriedly interred. From the Latin *sanitas*, health.

Sap. A short **trench** branching out from a main trench. Technically, a trench was dug *down*wards, into the earth, a sap was dug *out*wards, from within. See also, **Latrine**.

Sap head. The business end of a **sap**, often a shell hole turned into an **O-Pip**.

Sapper. A soldier in the **R. E.**, Royal Engineers. From the Latin *sappa*, a spade.

Saturday night soldier. See **Terrier**.

Sausage. An observation balloon. It was shaped like a bloated sausage and was non-dirigible, i.e. it could not be steered. Sausages were filled with hydrogen and raised and lowered by a steel rope attached to a winch. Its observer watched enemy lines from a wicker basket, communicating by buzzer with the **artillery** below, identifying targets for them and correcting the fall of fire. 'What time is the balloon going up?' was used throughout the Army to mean 'When do we start?' Administratively, sausages came under the control of the **Royal Flying Corps.** but it was usual for at least one of the observers to be an artillery officer with the **wind** up. Also known as Randy Richard or Maiden's delight, from a perceived resemblance to the engorged male member.

Sausage eater, sausage monger. An epithet for **Jerry**, after his alleged favourite food, *wurst*, sausage. The phrase 'gone to Sausage Hill' referred to someone who had been captured and put in a German prisoner of war camp.

Sawn-off. The correct military adjective for the shortened version of any item. Thus, a **donk** was a sawn-off horse, a **bantam** was a sawn-off soldier.

Scene shifter. A piece of heavy **artillery**. From its effectiveness in rearranging the scenery prior to a **show**.

Scrounge. To purloin another's kit or comestibles without permission. Since kit was always going missing, and since to be short of kit was a military **crime**, scrounging was endemic throughout the Army. See also, **Win**.

Seam squirrel. A louse. See also, **Chat**, **Prussian Guard**.

Self-inflicted wound. A wound inflicted by a man upon himself in the hope of evading combat. Desperate men would shoot themselves 'accidentally', or get others to do it for them, after first wrapping hands or feet in blankets to stop **muzzle flash** scorching their skin. Another method was to hold one's limbs above the **parapet** in the hope of attracting the aim of a **sniper**. Diseases could also be simulated. Inhaling smoke before a medical examination could give a man palpitations. Drugs like digitalis disturbed the circulation. Scraped tonsils suggested a man was coughing blood. See also, **Malinger**.

Sentry. A soldier ordered to stay alert and keep watch for the enemy. To fall asleep while on **sentry go** was punishable by execution. The total number of British sentries executed on the **Western Front** for sleeping at their posts was two.

Sentry go. The length of time for which a man was posted as **sentry**, usually two hours. Also known as 'doing stag'.

'Separate peace.' A man reaching his limits of endurance would sometimes talk about making a separate peace with the enemy.

Separation allowance. The money paid by the government to a soldier's family after he had joined the Army. The amount varied according to the soldier's rank and the number of children he had.

The wife of a **private** with no children got 12s/6d per week. The wife of a **sergeant** with three children got £1.10s. Each child under 14 was worth three shillings. The allowance was paid on Tuesdays at Post Offices.

Sepoy. An Indian **infantry private** in the Indian Army. See also, **Naik**.

Sergeant. In an **infantry battalion**, the sergeant was the **N.C.O.** attached to the **subaltern** in charge of a **platoon**. From the Latin *servire*, to serve.

Sergeant major, S.M. A senior **sergeant**, nickname 'the major'. In an **infantry battalion** there was one sergeant major per **company**, to assist its **captain**. The S.M.'s badge of rank was his three **chevrons**, plus a crown. **Sergeant major** also referred to the crown symbol in **Crown and Anchor**.

Severely handled. An officer's understatement to describe heavy **casualties**.

'Shabash!' Well done! Persian derivation. Among troops who had served in India *shabash* could also be used sarcastically to draw attention to a mistake or accident.

Shag. Compressed, tarry tobacco, mainly for pipe smokers. See **Plug**.

'Share that among you!' An invitation to accompany the lobbing of a **Mills bomb**, especially one tossed into a **Jerry dug-out** during **mopping up**. See also, *Kamerad*.

Shave. A rumour emanating from the barber.

Sheep dip. Medicine, lotion. Also a disparagement of any unpleasant drink.

Shell shock. An incapacitating nervous reaction to the trauma of battle. **M.O.**s tried to distinguish between two types of shell shock: that caused by being blown up and that caused by psychological stress. When officers had it the word 'neurasthenia' was used.

Shemozzle. A noisy argument, a **rear-up** or **tamasha**.

Shiny arse. A clerk polishing the seat of his uniform on a stool at a desk.

Shock absorber. A pilot's sarcasm for his **observer**.

Shoey. The blacksmith.

Shop. Stale talk about the war or the Army. Talking shop was banned in the **mess**, along with talk about religion, known women and politics.

Short arm parade. A **sick parade** to inspect men for symptoms of venereal disease, 'short arm' being one of **Tommy**'s nicknames for his member. See also, **Clap**, **Phyllis**.

Show. A military enterprise, a **stunt**. Show alludes to the entertainment value of any raid or attack to the **red tabs** responsible for staging it. To put on a good show was to secure the objective or fight honourably. A bad show was a missed opportunity or bungled effort.

Shrapnel, shrap. A shell filled with balls of lead for use primarily against **infantry** but also, for want of something better, to break up barbed wire. From its inventor, General Henry Shrapnel (died 1842). The shrapnel shell of a British eighteen-pounder contained 374 lead balls. The jagged pieces scattered when a shell exploded were splinters not shrapnel.

Sick parade. The daily gathering of men reporting as too sick for duty. In the event of a man being judged by the **M.O.** to be genuinely ill he would be marked down as excused duty. Otherwise, he would be given a **Number nine pill** and assigned to **light duties**, meaning **fatigues**. See also, **'Sixty-four, ninety-four.'**

Signal. Army jargon for a message.

Signalese. The language used by Army **signallers**, specifically, the coded alphabet they used which became part of Army vernacular: A – Ack; B – Beer; D – Don; M – Emma; P – Pip; S – Esses; T – Toc;

V – Vic. Hence, *Toc Emma* = TM = Trench Mortar. *Emma Gee* = MG = Machine Gun.

Signaller. A specialist in sending and receiving messages. Each **infantry battalion** started the war with 16 signallers. See also, **Buzz**, **Flag-wagger**.

Signs, the. Symbols introduced during 1916 to distinguish British armies, corps and **divisions** on the grounds that an image was more readily recognised than the written word and less helpful to a spy. Most signs had a hidden meaning. The sign of the 36th Division, comprising Protestant volunteers from Northern Ireland, was the Red Hand (of Ulster). The sign of the 56th Division, comprising London regiments, was Wat Tyler's sword.

Silent death. A patrol sent to lurk in **No Man's Land** in order to ambush a **Jerry** working party. It was silent because the weapons used were the cosh and the dagger.

'Sing! Sing! Or show us your ring!' The lewd instruction howled at nervous performers at any impromptu entertainment in **trench** or **billet**. The performer had to do a turn or drop his trousers. See also, **Gaff, 'Napoleon's greeting to his troops!'**

Sitter. Medical jargon. When it came to allocating places in **dhoolie wagons** and ambulance trains, **casualties** were either sitters or liers, a sitter being able to sit, a lier being a recumbent, one who had to be kept flat.

Six-bob-a-day tourists. A jealous British nickname for the **ANZACs**, after their arrival on the **Western Front** from Gallipoli. An **Aussie**'s basic pay was six times the one shilling (a bob) per day paid to a **Tommy**.

Six by four. Lavatory paper. From the dimensions, in inches, of each sheet of hard tissue. Scraps of it blowing about were called **trench** butterflies. See also, **Bumf**.

'Sixty-four, ninety-four.' The bugle call for **sick parade**, based on a mythical **Tommy**'s **regimental number**, 6494. 'Sixty-four, ninety-four/ Won't go sick any more/ the poor **bugger**'s dead.'

Skilly. Thin, unappetising Army stew. Also, the contents of a can of **bully** cooked with other ingredients such as onions or cabbage.

Skirt, a bit of. A young woman. See also, **Click**.

Skirt patrol. The collective noun for a group of soldiers in search of **skirt**.

Sky pilot. A military chaplain. See also, **Devil dodger**, **Padre**.

Slacker. A newspaper term for a non-volunteer, one staying at home.

Sling the bat. To talk the local language.

Smudged. Killed, rubbed out.

Snaffle. To steal.

Snip. A nickname for the tailor. See also, **Dersie**.

Snipe hole. A **sniper**'s place of vantage. It might be fitted with a steel shield with a loophole.

Sniper. A marksman detailed to **pick off** the enemy from concealment. Snipers messed separately and were excused **parades**, as were bombers and machine gunners.

Sniperscope. A wooden framework for sighting and firing a rifle so that the aimer didn't have to show himself above the **parapet** of his **trench**. Sniperscopes were **trench stores**, not the specialist tools of **snipers**. They could be fitted to **emma gees** as well as rifles.

Soldier's farewell. A parting curse. 'Fare ye well and f— the lot of you!'

Soldier's friend. His rifle. Also, a ubiquitous brand of brass polish. The phrase was used so often during the war as an advertising slogan it became a military sarcasm.

Somewhere in France. A phrase intended to preserve secrecy where the location of individual men and their units was concerned. From press censorship. Anyone on active service was forbidden to say where he was in his letters.

Sortie. A scouting mission, especially one undertaken by cavalry or aircraft. From the French *sortie*, exit. See also, **Recce**.

S.O.S. A signal for help in the form of an **artillery barrage**. On the telegraph, in **Morse code**, the S.O.S. signal was dot dot dot – dash dash dash – dot dot dot. The S.O.S. could also be sent by rockets in various colour combinations. During food shortages in Britain from 1917 onwards, S.O.S. became Save Or Starve.

Sound ranging, sound banging. A system for detecting **Jerry** guns by using acoustic and mathematical observations to determine their distance and direction. The other main way of finding enemy **artillery** was to plot the flashes when their guns fired.

Soup. Water in a shell hole flavoured by corpses or other battlefield debris.

Souvenir. A wound. Also, a battlefield trophy. Favourite items included brass shell fuses, buttons, badges, etc. Souvenir also referred to a baby born after its mother had **clicked** with a **Tommy**.

Sparks, to get the. To fire into **Jerry**'s barbed wire in order to get the range of his **trench**. Bullets hitting the wire would send up sparks.

Split-arse cap. The cap worn in the **Royal Flying Corps** when it finally got around to designing its own uniform. It was a type of glengarry, worn sideways on the head.

Spokey. A wheelwright, the skilled worker who fixed the wheels on Army wagons.

Sportsman's battalions. The 23rd and 24th Battalions, Royal Fusiliers, two London outfits allowed to recruit men up to the age of

45, thereby attracting ranchers, planters and game hunters from the distant corners of the Empire.

Spree. A celebratory night out. From the Gaelic *spreidh*, a cattle raid.

Spud. Potato. Also, the nickname of any man called Murphy. Also, a **Mills bomb**.

Spud adjutant. The **lance jack** put in charge of the potato-peeling **fatigue**.

Squadron. A sub-unit of a cavalry **regiment**, six officers and 150 men commanded by a **major**. On the **Western Front** the cavalry fought mostly on foot. In the **Royal Flying Corps**, a squadron was made up of flights, with five or six aircraft in each flight. An air squadron was also commanded by a major.

WILLS'S CIGARETTES.

A TRIBUTE TO THE TANKS

Squirt. A short burst of fire from an **emma gee**. See also, **Hose**.

S.R.D. The initials on the earthenware jars used for distributing **rum** in the **trenches**. The regulation **issue** was one tablespoonful dispensed by a **sergeant** under the supervision of an officer. S.R.D. was variously taken to mean Service Ration Depot, Service Rum Diluted, State Rum Distillery, Soon Run Dry, Seldom Reaches Destination, etc., etc. See also, **Tot**.

Staff. Officers whose job involved management, administration and planning rather than fighting in the field. Staff officers worked mainly behind the lines and were distinguished from regimental officers, or **regimentals**, by the wearing of a scarlet cap band and **red tabs**. Every general in the chain of command was served by a staff. From the Dutch *staf*, German *stab*, baton of rank. The French badge for a staff officer was an armband decorated with lightning bolts.

Stalhelm. The **Jerry** steel helmet. Known by a variety of nicknames including *waschbecken*, washbasin, *brocknfanger*, dustbin and *nachpott*, chamber pot. It came in six sizes so a snug fit was assured. **Tommy** called it a coal scuttle.

'Stand up to the bowling.' An officer's phrase intended to encourage men to face heavy fire. Derived from the cricket pitch.

Starvation corner. The place at the **mess** table that was served last.

Sticky Jack. A special envelope, also known as a **green envelope**, for private correspondence. The correspondent licked and stuck down the flap himself instead of giving his letter to an officer to be censored and sealed.

Stiff's paddock. Cemetery. See also, **Rest camp**.

Stink pot. An empty can filled with excrement and thrown, or fired by catapult, in **Jerry**'s general direction. A feature of the early days of **trench** warfare. Retaliation in kind was inevitable, leading to the weapon being abandoned by mutual consent. See also, **Jam tin**.

Stockings and suspenders. The harness of **webbing** from which a **footslogger** hung his kit.

Stokes. See **Hand Cart Cavalry**, **Trench mortar**.

Stonk, stonker. To smash and make useless, applied to both men and machines. Derived from the Italian *stanco*, exhausted.

Stragglers post. A place behind the battle line where **red caps** kept an eye open for potential deserters trying to sneak to the rear. Also where **Jerry** prisoners were handed over for safe keeping.

Stretcher bearer. Each **infantry battalion** had 16 stretcher bearers, usually musicians in the regimental band. Also known as **bodysnatchers** or **dhoolie wallahs**.

Stripe. See **Chevron**.

Stunt. See **Show**.

Sturmpanzerkampfwagen. A **Jerry** tank, introduced in 1918. It was a ridiculous, lumbering affair, 26 feet long and 32 tons in weight, into which were crammed 18 men and six machine guns. Only about 20 of them were made.

Subaltern, sub. A second lieutenant or a **lieutenant**. He was paid 7s/6d per day, about enough for one bottle of whisky. From the Latin *subalternus*, succeeding in turn.

Suicide club. Any squad given a dangerous assignment. Bombers and machine gunners applied the term to themselves as an honorific.

Survey, the. See **Field Survey**.

Sweating on it. To await an event with anticipation or apprehension. The more **Tommy** wanted something – **leaf**, a promotion, his next letter from home – the more he was said to be sweating on it. 'Sweating on the line' was the **Bingo** term for when a player had all his numbers in a line except the one he needed to win.

Swede. The correct Army word for a turnip. The **Jock** word for swedes was neeps.

Swede basher. A soldier from the West of England, where the growing of turnips was assumed to be part of the way of life.

Swing it down the line. To **wangle** a job at the **base**.

Swing the lead. To **malinger**.

Sword. The correct term for a **bayonet** in a rifle **regiment**.

IS FOR

**TEMPORARY
GENTLEMAN**

HQ, 198th Infantry Brigade,
British Expeditionary Force,
27th April, 1916.

Dear Edward,

Chateau life is _cushy_ alright but the work itself is
mundane in the extreme. Mostly I am employed on
the sort of clerical duties any schoolboy could master,
making lists and summaries of various daily reports
and labelling them correctly.

I saw Connery today, by chance, and he gave a
glowing account of how the Fighting Fifth's latest
reinforcements are shaping up. The old _batt_ is almost
back to strength under a new colonel and raring for
another tilt at Brother _Bosche_. War these days is no
longer a purely professional affair to be settled by the
regulars. Major Gaunt is a case in point. He is by
no means a stupid or lazy man but cannot accept
anyone as a _pukka_ officer without a social pedigree
and a commanding way with inferiors. _Rankers_
he can tolerate since they know their place but the
amateur soldier who was a bank clerk or schoolmaster
in _Civvy Street_ – well, it is a question of breeding.
A civilian in uniform might learn to talk and act
like an officer but he can never be a gentleman, only
temporary.

The reception Gaunt gave our latest addition to
the _mess_ was unpardonably rude. His name is Taylor
and he talks with a pronounced agricultural accent,

notwithstanding the fact that he is a well set-up type
of chap and clearly able to handle himself, as evidenced
by the purple and white ribbon on his chest. Given the
quantity of _temporary gents_ reaching the _Front_ these
days one would have thought Gaunt might have been
up to the challenge. 'You the new _wart_?' he growled,
when Taylor was introduced. 'Brought any _pish_ with
you?'

No one had told Taylor, of course, that newly
arrived _subalterns_ were meant to bring whisky with
them for their first toast to the _Brigade_. In matters
of _regimental_ form, the Army expects its officers to
know without being told. 'No whisky?' fumed Gaunt.
'Where's the _bloody_ use in that?' The poor unfortunate
Taylor only made matters worse by offering to
share half a sack of apples from his father's farm.
Someone had told him, quite rightly, that we are
all starved of fresh fruit. 'Apples?' scowled Gaunt,
tipping out the sack and stamping on the contents.
'Mouldy old apples!? It's pish we need, boy. Pish, pish
and more pish. Not bloody cider!' Imagine winning
the _M.C._ and being welcomed like that. Young Taylor's
worth ten of Gaunt in the sort of _show_ we are about
to put on. But _hush_.
All in good time.

     I'll write again soon.
     Yours ever,

     Chaz

Tadpole tail. An extension fitted to the back of a **tank** to enable it to cross wide **trenches**. From the tadpole, whose tail falls off when it is ready to be a frog.

Take a powder. To take one's medicine. Sarcastically, to flee danger as if having taken a laxative. See also, **Castor Oil Dragoons**.

Take the stripe. To accept a promotion as **N.C.O.** Many men declined promotion in order to stay with their **muckers**.

'Take your hat off in the House of the Lord . . . you heathen bastard!' An **N.C.O.**'s witticism for use during **church parade**. The first part was whispered reverentially but the punchline was spat out with venom.

Tank. A **wet canteen**. To get tanked-up was to drink to the limit of one's capacity.

Tank. Codeword for the armoured **landship** first used in battle during the Somme Offensive, 15 September 1916. To preserve secrecy they were transported to France as water tanks. A tank was either male or female. The male carried two small cannon and four machine guns. The female tank carried six machine guns. Each tank weighed 28 tons and had a maximum speed over good ground of 4 mph. By the end of the war, the Army had more than 3,000 tanks in the field. The effect on **Jerry** is conveyed by his word *tankschrecken*, tank-fear. His word for tank was *schützengrabenvernichtungautomobil* which means roughly motor-powered fire-trench exterminator.

Tanner. A silver sixpence, worth about one French **frong**.

Tannergram. A telegram. Also, facetious for a military signal. From the minimum cost of sending one in **Blighty**.

Tell off. To give a section or **platoon** its instructions. To tell off the **sentry** was to give him the password and identify his post. From tell, to count.

Temporary gentleman. A **civvy** granted an officer's **commission** for the **duration**.

Terps. An interpreter on loan from the French army. He wore a golden sphinx on his collar, as devised by Napoleon during his Egyptian campaign. It was a standing joke that no one could understand a word he said.

Terrier. A soldier in the Territorial Force, created in 1908. Terriers were part-timers who trained at nights and at weekends, hence **Saturday night soldiers**. They took part in manoeuvres with regulars once a year. Territorial units were not obliged to fight overseas, they had to volunteer, which most of them did. **Red tabs** and regulars tended to look down on terriers but during the spring of 1915 they became the main source of British manpower for the **Western Front**.

Third man. A specific superstition of smokers. It was universally held true in Army **joss** that misfortunes came in threes and that the third man to light his **fag** from the same **lucifer** would be hit by a **sniper**'s bullet. The first light drew the sniper's attention; the second light gave him the range; the third light was his target.

Three parts five eighths. Tipsy but not fully drunk.

Thruster. A keen, aggressive officer with his eye on promotion. From the characteristically pushy behaviour of well-mounted riders in the chase.

Thunderbox. A commode. A boxed-in convenience. See also, **Latrine**.

Tic tac. A **signaller**. See also, **Buzz**, **Flag-wagger**, **Iddy umpty**.

Ticket. Discharge from the Army in the event of incapacity. Also, the **chit** more properly known as the field medical card pinned onto a battlefield **casualty**. A **leaf** ticket authorised **Tommy** to go on leave. A man with a one-way ticket had felt a premonition of death. See also, **Cold meat ticket**.

Tickler. The name of the Army's chief jam supplier. One tin of Tickler's **plum and apple** was the standard issue of **pozzie** for a section of **infantry**. Tickler also made jam out of rhubarb. A **bomb** improvised in an old jam tin was known as a tickler.

Ticklish. The Army adjective for any piece of work requiring care and attention.

Tiger. Georges Clemençeau, the aggressive French Prime Minister from 1917 onwards. 'Home policy? I wage war. Foreign policy? I wage war. All the time I wage war.'

Tin can. A **tank**.

Tin fish. A submarine.

Tin lid. The British steel helmet, the **battle bowler**.

Tinned dog. Unidentifiable meat. See also, **Pickled monkey**.

Toasting fork. A bayonet.

Toe parade. Foot inspection. See also, **Trench foot**, **Whale oil**.

Toffee apple. A type of **trench mortar** bomb. It was the size of a **football** attached to a stalk. When the bomb was fired its stalk went whizzing through the air separately, sometimes landing whence it came. **Dud** toffee apples were sometimes emptied of their explosive and used as **gas gongs**.

Tommy. The British **private**. From Thomas Atkins, the name of a private soldier in Wellington's army, taken as a specimen for the purpose of demonstrating how to fill in Army forms. **Frogs**, **Jerries**, **Aussies** and **Yanks** all addressed the British soldier as Tommy. By association, Tommy came to stand for the whole British Army and, as adjective, anything British. Tommy rarely used the word himself, except with self-deprecation, pity or irony.

WILLS'S CIGARETTES.

A TRIBUTE TO THE MACHINE GUN CORPS.

'Toot sweet!' Quickly! Do it now! Tommy's French. From *toute de suite*, at once. 'Do it toot sweet, lads, and the tooter the sweeter.' See also, **'Alley toot sweet!'**

Tot. The measure for issuing rum, 1/64th of a gallon per man. See also, **S.R.D.**

Toy shop. A dump for weapons and kit.

Toys. Military equipment used in training. Also, new or prototype weaponry.

Tracer. A bullet made visible in flight by a phosphorescent compound that left a trail of smoke in daylight and glowed in the dark. Tracer bullets were inserted at regular intervals in belts of machine gun ammunition to show the angle of fire and so help aiming. Also applied to incendiary bullets used against **sausages** and **Zepps**. By inserting a tracer near the end of a belt of ammunition, a machine gunner had a visual reminder that it would soon be time to reload.

Travelling circus. A **trench mortar** or machine gun team roaming from **trench** to trench to hit **Jerry** before moving on. Travelling circuses were very unpopular because their activities always brought retaliation on the local garrison. The phrase could also apply to an inspection by **brass hats**. The most famous travelling circus on the **Western Front** was the **squadron** of aircraft led by the German **ace**, Manfred von Richthofen, the Red Baron.

Traverse. The kink built into a **trench** so that in the event of **Jerry** penetration he could not fire along its whole length. Traverses also helped to localise damage from shellfire. In a **fire trench**, the sections between traverses were called fire bays.

Travesty. A badly dug or incompetently sited **traverse**.

Tray beans. Very well. **Tommy**'s French. From *très bien*.

Tray bong. Very good. From *très bon*.

Trek. A march. From the Dutch of South Africa via the Boer War, 1899–1902.

Trench. An excavation for shelter or defence. From the French *trancher*, to cut.

Trench fever. Commonly diagnosed as P.U.O., Pyrexia of Unknown Origin, on medical forms. Symptoms included high temperature, dizziness and vomiting. The transmission of trench fever was eventually tracked down to the excrement of **chats** getting into the human blood stream through scratched skin.

Trench foot. Badly swollen feet caused by standing in freezing water for hours on end. Trench foot was a serious cause of manpower **wastage** during the winter of 1914–15. The rubbing on of **whale oil** was prescribed as a treatment.

Trench mortar. A compact artillery piece for lobbing bombs. The best British trench mortar was the **Stokes**. See also, **Football Cavalry**, **Hand Cart**, **Minnie**.

Trench nomenclature. The correct jargon for the naming of trenches and other features of the **Line**. For maps of the battlefield to make sense, every trench had to be named or numbered. Some were named colloquially by the units who dug them, others were named alphabetically by the **staff**. See also, **Field Survey**, **Pimple**.

Trench stores. Items of equipment kept permanently in the trenches, e.g. **banjos**, **micks**, **Very lights**, **gas curtains**, **Ayrton fans**, etc. Trench stores were handed over from one unit to the next on **relief**, and had to be accounted for with an **ident**.

Tripe. A tri-plane, one with three wings.

Tripe roared out. A severe telling off.

Troop. A sub-unit of a cavalry **squadron**, equivalent to an **infantry platoon**. From the French *troupeau*, herd. Trooper was **Tommy**'s word for a cavalryman.

Trots, the. Diarrhoea. If it got worse it became the **gallops**.

Trusty Triumph. The Army's favoured motorcycle, the Triumph Model H roadster, as used by a despatch rider, or Don R in **Signalese**. The firm of Triumph was founded and managed by a German, Siegfried Bettman, who set up in Coventry in 1884, first as a bike seller, later as a manufacturer. By the end of the war some 20,000 Triumphs had been bought by the British and another 10,000 by their **Allies**.

Turd walloper. A man assigned to the **sanitary squad**.

'Turn up the wick!' More light, please!

Typewriter. Machine gun. From the sound of it. See also, **Mangle**.

Tyro. A newcomer, a **rookie**. From the Latin *tiro*, army recruit.

U

IS FOR

UNSTUCK

5th West Kent Fusiliers,
British Expeditionary Force,
10th May, 1916.

Dear Nephers,

   Thank you for the latest letters from you and
the kneesers. I enjoy reading them very much so
keep them coming. The drawings this time were
very good indeed. I am writing separately because
I do not think the girls would be interested in the
answer to your question about which <u>artillery</u>
shells kill the most men. There are three types:
<u>heavies, shrapnel</u> and gas. Heavies are full of
high explosive, a chemical mixture that makes
things go bang. The bigger the shell the bigger the
bang. <u>Jerry's</u> heavies go off with an enormous
bang in a cloud of smelly black smoke. <u>Tommy</u>
calls them <u>Woolly Bears</u> or <u>Jack Johnsons</u>. The gas
shells hardly make any sound. That makes them
especially dangerous. But we usually manage to
get our <u>respirators</u> on in time. The third type of
shell is shrapnel. It explodes in the air and sends
hundreds of bullets lashing down. The heavies come
trundling through the air quite slowly, which gives
us a few seconds' warning. Their job is to blow up
trenches and buildings. Shrapnel arrives much
quicker. Its job is to stop men in their tracks.
Even so, if we crouch down under our <u>tin lids,</u> it

does not do too much damage. The important thing is, and you must keep this quite secret, it is a deady secret, we are getting up more _guns_ than ever and Jerry had better watch out because pretty soon he is going to find out just how good they are!

Thank you once again for you letter and please note my change of address. Tell your father also. In fact, show him this letter, please, except for the secret bit.

Very best regards to you both,
    your affectionate uncle,

Charles Cartwright,
Lieutenant, Active Service,
Signed on the battlefield.

(Edward, a chance came up to get back to the old _batt_ and since the immediate future for _infantry_ looks quite interesting I took it. I think you will understand if I explain that my speedy return to _regimental_ duties enjoyed Major Gaunt's enthusiastic encouragement from first to last. When I got back here the _Adj_ was even able to arrange a berth for me in my original _Company_, the 'Capital C'. I could not be happier. Best, C.)

U-boat. A **Jerry** submarine. From *unterseeboot*, under-sea boat. The Royal Navy sank more than 200 of them. See also, **Tin fish**.

Ubique. Everywhere. From Latin. The motto of the Royal Artillery, the **gunners**, and the Royal Engineers, the **sappers**. Because of their ubiquity in every campaign, units in these regiments did not receive battle honours.

Umpty iddy. To feel unwell. **Signaller**'s slang. From the reversal of **iddy umpty**.

Umpty poo. A little bit more. *Tommy*'s French. From *un petit peu*, a little more.

Uncle Sam. See **Doughboy**, **Yank**.

Unconsumed portion. That part of the day's ration a soldier was ordered or allowed to reserve for later consumption. Colloquially, the phrase could refer to anything left over. If a battery of **guns** had shells remaining after destroying its target, they comprised its unconsumed portion. See also, **Afters**.

Undertaker's squad. Stretcher bearers, the **dhoolie wallahs**. See also, **Bodysnatcher**.

Unhealthy. Dangerous. The adjective for a place under accurate **Jerry** observation.

Unstuck. To come unstuck was to be found out. Also, to be demoted in rank.

Up. The **Front**, the upmost of which was the **fire trench**. Up was the opposite of Down, the **base**, the basest of which was the gangplank of a boat heading for **Blighty**. At any given moment, every **Tommy** knew exactly how far Up or Down he might be.

Up there. Brains. The phrase was usually accompanied by a tap on the forehead. 'It's up there you want it, my lad . . .'

IS FOR

VERMOREL

5th West Kent Fusiliers,
British Expeditionary Force,
6th June, 1916.

Dear Mudge and Fudge,

We are training ferociously but that did not
stop me getting to a school reunion two days ago,
organised by one of the chaps I worked with at
<u>Brigade</u> when I was doing my <u>staff</u> learning. It
turned out to be a most tonic antidote to slogging
about the French countryside on <u>route marches</u> and
<u>field days</u>, which has been our lot for the past couple
of weeks. The <u>Old Sweats</u> have seen it all before.
They know we are being <u>fattened up</u> for the <u>big
Push</u>, which gives them ample scope for terrorising
the <u>rookies</u>. Our new colonel, Beardsley, was in
the Coldstream before the war and has brought
some much-appreciated point and decision to our
somewhat casual ways. The men love him.

As for Founders Day, when the three of us
from our Brigade arrived at the hotel in <u>Ameens</u>
we found two <u>brass hats</u> in the stable yard,
organising the younger elements for a proper
game of football. We managed a good half hour.
And it did feel good to get down to a serious scrap
after several games recently of what the lads call
soccer. An <u>artillery captain</u> I recognised from
Lubbock's, called Allot, scored two excellent shot

goals for us and we came out on top, two points to one, despite our behinds being pretty ropey, especially when I was put in for a spell to catch my wind after a flattening. This war plays havoc with one's fitness for a good old-fashioned ruck. Afterwards, having worked up an appetite, our generals presided at a dinner. They led us in the Carmen after which we toasted absent friends. It struck us all, I think, how for some present it was certain to be their last Fourth on earth. We returned well after midnight, singing our heads off. It was one of the jolliest joy rides I have had out here and left me feeling thoroughly bucked. Floreat Etona et Alma Domus.

Yours till the cows come home,

Charles

V.A.D., Voluntary Aid Detachment. Provided nursing services during the war both in the field and back in **Blighty**. See also, **Fanny**, **Field ambulance**.

Valise. An officer's sleeping bag, made of blanket on the inside and waterproof canvas on the outside. Also used to refer to an officer's kit bag. See also, **Fart sack**, **Flea bag**.

Valroy water. Mineral water bottled under the supervision of the E. F. C., Expeditionary Force Canteens. Its source was the Valroy spring near **Eat Apples**. The same factory also made the Army's soda water, ginger ale and cordial.

Vamp. An alluring woman, a seducer, the grown-up cousin of a **flapper**.

V.C., Victoria Cross. The highest British award for **gallantry**, instituted by Queen Victoria, 1856, and made of bronze from Russian cannon captured during the Crimean War.

V.C. mixture. Rum. See **S.R.D.**

Vedette. A **sentry** on a horse. From the Latin *videre*, to see.

Ventilate. To smash buildings with **artillery** to improve their airflow. Also applied to the state of one's uniform after combat. See also, **Daylight**.

Vermijelli. A mixture of oil, soap and water for killing **chats**. Manufactured by Messrs Bowley & Sons, of Battersea, London. Vermijelli was also **Tommy**'s pronunciation of the Belgian village of Voormezeele.

Vermorel sprayer. A hand-operated pump-syringe connected to a churn of chemicals carried on the back. The Vermorel was invented for spraying garden flowers with insecticide but on the **Western Front** it was adapted to spray hypo compound to disperse gas in **trenches**.

Very light. A rocket used as a **signal** flare. Green, yellow, red or white flares sent coded messages to the **artillery**. From the name of its inventor, often mis-spelled as Verey.

Vesta. A match, for lighting a **fag**. From the chaste Roman goddess whose flame was kept permanently alight by the Vestal virgins.

Vickers. The heavy British machine gun, mounted on a tripod. From the firm that made it. The Vickers could fire 400–600 bullets per minute, about the same as thirty men with rifles. At that rate, the Vickers' barrel became hot very quickly so it was fitted with a cylindrical jacket cooled by water. Sustained firing boiled the water, which was unhelpful if the steam revealed the gun's position.

Virgin of the Limp. A gilded statue on the main church in the ruined French town of Albert. The Virgin was officially known as Notre Dame de Brebières.Visible for miles around, she became a symbol of the Battle of the Somme, July–November 1916, which ended with a million casualties on both sides. See **Lady of the Limp**.

Volte-face. To turn straight round and head back to the start. An unheroic but not entirely uncommon manoeuvre. From the Italian *volta faccia*, turn face.

Von Kluck. The first **Jerry** general to engage the **B.E.F.**, at Mons, Belgium, 23 August 1914. His name offered **Tommy** a lewd rhyme for his marching songs although in German the name was pronounced Fon Klook. He was wounded in 1915, retired in 1916.

IS FOR

WHITE
HOPE

5th West Kent Fusiliers,
British Expeditionary Force,
20th June, 1916.

Dear Edward,

   I am under instructions from the platoon
to thank Lilly most profusely for the tablets of
writing paper, etcetera in her last parcel. The
bob-a-day most of them get as their wage is paid
out infrequently and when there is a pay parade
the most urgent call on their precious onks is a
bon tom. Stationery is one of the lowest items
on Tommy's shopping list, although one sheet
per man is usually enough. I have just finished
censoring the latest batch of their letters. Some
of them write absolute rot. One of the new lads has
described in gory detail a raid that never happened.
It is a complete work of fiction. We have not
been near old Jerry for at least a fortnight. Our
Division has been earmarked for close support,
to exploit any success on the big day, of which
expectations are high. I am not giving away
secrets. It is all in the Continental Daily Mail if
one can read between the lines. Jerry knows we are
coming, not the exact date, that's all. His guns
are concentrating on our communications and
artillery. Letters will be rather terse from now on,
I am afraid. We have hardly any time to ourselves

except to <u>kip</u>, and there's precious little of that.
As usual we will be <u>going over</u> in a state of near
exhaustion. Never mind.

Keep the home fires burning, old son,

Chazzer

Wagger. A **signaller**. From **flag-wagger**. See also, **Iddy umpty**.

'Waiter!' A summons tossed at **Jerry trenches** in the hope that a former German waiter would pop his head obediently above his **parapet**. An officer's jocularity. See **Kellner**.

Waler. A sturdy horse originally bred in the Australian state of New South Wales and esteemed for its stamina and resilience. See also, **Charger**.

Walking wounded, walkers. Soldiers who had **copped one** but were still able to get to the **poultice wallopers** on their own. See also, **Sitter**.

Wallah. A widely applied suffix meaning man, servant, assistant, specialist, owner or occupant. As in base-wallah, gas-wallah, post-wallah, etc. From the Hindustani *vala*, doer.

Wallop. Beer.

Walloons. French-speaking **Belgies** as opposed to the **Dutch** ones.

Wangle. To secure something by stealth or subterfuge and get away with it.

War baby. The youngest member of any unit. Especially applied to fresh **warts**. Also used to refer to **Tommy**'s illegitimate offspring.

War bond. A government bond issued to fund the war. Buying them was considered to be a patriotic duty.

War bread. As food shortages hit the belligerent nations, wheat flour became increasingly expensive and proportions of inferior substitutes – cornmeal, oatmeal, dried potato – replaced it in the baking of bread.

War bride. A woman marrying a soldier while he was on **leaf**.

War House. The War Office in London. A term of familiarity used by **red tabs**.

War Pictorial. A propaganda news sheet scattered by balloons over **Jerry**'s lines.

Warm. Dangerous. A favourite officers' understatement.

Warm up. A diversionary attack before the main assault. From the music hall, where lesser acts were sent on to get the audience into a receptive state for the eventual appearance of the star attraction. See also, **Scene shifter**, **Show**, **Stunt**.

Wart. A raw **subaltern**.

Wash-out. A failure, a **dud**. Applied equally to comrades or kit.

Wasserman test. The test applied to a blood sample to diagnose syphilis. See **Phyllis**.

Wastage. The steady, daily loss of manpower through **attrition**.

Waterloo day. Pay day. **Regular Army** derivation. See also, **Buckshee**.

Weak in the arm. Half a pint of beer in a pint pot. Cockney drinking slang. Also used as a complaint against short measure.

Webbing. A body harness of leather or thick canvas on which **Tommy** hung his ammunition pouches and other kit.

Webley. The main type of pistol issued to officers and some **N.C.O.**s. It fired six bullets from a revolving chamber.

Weevil. Any insect found in a **dog** biscuit.

'We'll soon lick you into shape . . .' The traditional welcoming phrase to a **rookie**.

Welsh cricket. A louse. See **Chat**.

Welsh Wizard. A newspaper nickname given to David Lloyd George as minister of munitions and then, from December 1916 until the end of the war, as Prime Minister of a coalition government. On the

Western Front it was likely to be used ironically.

West, to go. To be killed. The phrase was also used to mean lost or **missing**. 'Anyone seen my **daisies**, they've gone west again?'

Western Front. Its length varied almost from month to month but on average it was 460 miles long. From 1916 onwards it was held, north to south, as follows: the **Belgies** held the first 10–15 miles, from the North Sea coast to **The Salient; Tommy** held the next stretch, from north of **Eeps** down to the River Somme and slightly beyond; the **Frogs** held the rest, down to the Swiss border. The British **Line** was longest in March 1918, when it measured 123 miles, from the Houthulst Forest in Belgium to St Gobain in France.

Westerner. A **frock** or **brass hat** who believed in concentrating the British military effort on the **Western Front** because that was where **Jerry** was strongest and therefore the only place where a decisive military victory would ensure his defeat. **Easterners** argued that the Central Powers could be weakened to the point of collapse by attacks through the Balkans or the Black Sea. Wrangling between Westerners and Easterners continued throughout the war.

Wet. A drink. When an **N.C.O.** was promoted it was obligatory for his comrades to arrange a beano so they could wet his **stripe**.

Wet and a wad. Cup of tea and a bun.

Wet rations. Mud.

Whale oil. Melted down whale blubber, originally used as fuel for lamps. In **trenches** whale oil was rubbed into men's feet as a means of water-proofing them to prevent **trench foot**. Whale oil was also used by pilots to protect their faces from the bitter cold at high altitude.

'What's this one in aid of?' A question addressed to women and girls selling paper flags in aid of war charities. A **Blighty** phrase.

'Where did that one go?' A question heard frequently from anyone straightening himself after **bobbing** to avoid an **arrival**.

Whippet. A smaller, lighter type of **tank** than the ponderous **landship**. The whippet carried three men and three machine guns. It was meant to have a top speed of 8 mph and was nicknamed the **musical box**. See also, **Willie**.

Whistling Percy. An **arrival**. From the noise it made on descent.

White flag. The sign of surrender.

White hope. Anyone or anything from which much was expected. Derived from the search in the United States for a white boxer capable of beating **Jack Johnson**, the black heavyweight champion of the world.

White Sheet, White Shirt. The Belgian village of Wytschaete, south of **The Salient**.

Whizz-bang. The shell from a quick-firing field gun. The bang came almost simultaneously with the whizz of its approach. Also a slang term for a **field postcard**. See also, **Quick Dick**.

'Who called the cook a bastard?' The question asked whenever a soldier was presented with an unappetising meal, the implication being that it was deliberate revenge from the cook against someone questioning his paternity. The question might be answered grimly, after tasting, 'Who called the bastard a cook?' See also, **'Any complaints?'**

'Who's won?' The question sometimes asked at the end of a **stunt**.

'Who were you with last night?' The first line of a music-hall song quoted at any comrade jealously suspected of having **clicked**. 'Who were you with last night/ Under the pale moonlight/ It wasn't your sister/ It wasn't your ma . . ./ I saw yer, I saw yer . . .'

Whole skinned. The adjective to describe the uninjured. To emerge from a **stunt** whole skinned was to survive intact.

Wilkinson of Pall Mall. A well-known maker of **swords** for officers, incorporated 1889.

Willie. A nickname for **whippet**. See also, **Little Willie**.

Win. To acquire something without permission, to steal. See also, **Borrow**.

Wind windy. To have the wind up was to be frightened, quite reasonably, by the hazards of war. But **windy**, as an adjective, implied habitual fearfulness or unreliability. Windy in **trench nomenclature** – Windy Corner, Windy Lane – signified any place known to be very **unhealthy**, especially a crossroads. As a noun, a wind up meant a false alarm, as in 'We were warned he might be coming over but it was just another wind up.'

Windyberg Line. See **Hindenburg Line**.

Winning the war. The phrase used to greet any pointless order or disappointment. 'Seen the latest? We've got to pay for our own bootlaces – that's the way to win the war.'

Winter sports. **Trench** raids, imposed by the **staff** as an antidote to lethargy in the trenches. See also, **Garrison sports**.

Wipers. The Belgian town of Ypres, at the centre of its eponymous **Salient**. Pronounced Eeps or Eeprez in **Tommy**'s French. The pronunciation 'Wipers' was attributed to the first British **C-in-C**, Sir John French, who was notorious for his inability to 'parlay' **Frahnsay**.

Wire. Barbed wire, for defence against surprise attack. Also, among **signallers**, copper wire for carrying **signals**. Both types were carried on reels.

Wire tap. Signallers could use clips or knots to tap in to signal wires, either to intercept enemy messages or to send their own. Trade derivation, from plumbing.

Wooden cross. To be granted the Order of the Wooden Cross was to be killed and buried under one. See also, **Rest camp**, **Stiff's paddock**.

Wooden overcoat. Coffin.

Woodbine. Popular brand of **fag** made by the Bristol firm of W.D. & H.O. Wills. They came in packets or tins. Sometimes abbreviated to Woods, Woodies.

Woodbine Willie. Nickname of a Church of England padre, Geoffrey Studdert-Kennedy, who had the habit of pressing **Woodbines** on the wounded. His poems extolling the Christ-like forbearance of the fighting man earned him a wide readership. See also, **Padre**, **God botherer**, **Sky pilot**.

Woolly Bear. A German heavy shell that exploded in a dense cloud of black smoke. See also, **Jack Johnson**.

Working party. A group of **infantry** assigned to carry out physical labour under the supervision of the **sappers**. A working party was a more formal affair than a **fatigue**. It was carried out to suit the Army's wider purposes, not those of one's **battalion**.

Wound stripe. See, **Gold stripe**.

Wrist watch. During the course of the war the wrist watch steadily replaced the watch-and-chain. They were for officers rather than men, mainly because of the expense. Gold wrist watches went for £8, silver ones began at £2.10s. Highly prized as **souvenirs**.

Wullie. Sir William Robertson, Chief of the Imperial General Staff, who rose from private to field marshal. As a **Westerner** he was an ally of the Commander-in-Chief, Sir Douglas Haig. See **Ranker**.

IS FOR

X-DAY

5th West Kent Fusiliers,
British Expeditionary Force,
29th June, 1916.

Dear Mudge and Fudge,

The most appalling thing has happened. I have sprained my ankle really badly. I was on my rounds yesterday when I stepped back to avoid the water cart and trod in a bucket. My whole foot swelled up instantly like an elephant's. The pain, if I put the slightest strain on it, is excruciating. The M.O. had to cut my boot off to get at it. I limped back to the Transport lines on one boot and a stick. The M.O. says I will have to wait for the swelling to go down before he can see if I have wrecked it completely. It will almost certainly mean going under the knife again. In the meantime my place in 'C' Company is empty. I feel utterly wretched at being left out. The Fighting Fifth is heading into the biggest battle in history while I am sitting here unable to put on my own socks. It is the most appalling bad luck. Please send 2 pairs new boots urgently and make one a pair of size nines and the other a pair of elevens.

Your wretched son,

Charles

X. The Army numeral for 10. From the Romans. The Mark X of any weapon or piece of kit that was the tenth improved or modified version of it since first issue.

X-day. Two days to go until **Zero**.

Xylonite goggles. A mask of armoured steel to protect the eyes from shell splinters. The slits in these goggles were so narrow none of the eye could be seen from outside.

WILLS'S CIGARETTES.

GENERAL FOCH.

IS FOR

YEOMANRY

5th West Kent Fusiliers,
British Expeditionary Force,
1st July, 1916.

Dear Edward,

   The big _Push_ began about six hours ago without
me. I clearly heard our steady bombardment
intensifying to a crescendo, followed by the distinct
explosions of some mighty _mines._ Since then I
have only been able to gauge what is happening
from the sound of the guns and the somewhat
inscrutable ways of our aircraft overhead. Our
Division has not gone over yet, according to the
only scrap of _gup_ that has filtered back this far.
As far as we are concerned in the Transport, the
fog of war has descended completely.
   I am only writing because it gives me
something to do and I know one of the drivers is
going down to _Brigade_ shortly. Otherwise I would
be hobbling about ineffectually, talking to the _donks_
and cursing my fate. Now and then the thunder
of the guns surges and then dies down again. I
cannot tell what it means. In some ways this is
a very modern war, in others positively medieval.
No information comes back for hours once the lads
go over.
   (Later) The first _walking wounded_ have started
to come by, heading for the _field ambulance_ down

the lane. None of them could tell us anything definite. One of the <u>Jocks,</u> who was very happy to be out of it with a <u>fag</u> between his lips, said none of his <u>mob</u> had got close to <u>Jerry's wire.</u> Someone else said his <u>line</u> had been pounded out of sight and Brother <u>Bosche</u> was taking a real thrashing. No one knows anything for sure once the <u>barrage</u> lifts.

Yours uselessly,

Charles

'Y'. The Y.M.C.A., Young Men's Christian Association, an international organisation that ran rest huts and dry **canteens** in **rest** areas. Also known as the Y-Emma, from its first two initials when rendered into **Signalese**.

Yank. An American. From Yankee, the American Indian pronunciation of the French word, *Anglais*. See also, **A.E.F.**, **Doughboy**.

Yellow cross. Shells containing **mustard gas** in liquid form were marked with a yellow cross. See also, **Phosgene**.

Yellow girl. A munitionette, i.e. a female worker in a munitions factory. The chemicals she handled could turn her skin yellow.

Yeomanry. The cavalry arm of the **terriers**. From yeoman, the Anglo Saxon *gea-mann*, land man, a cultivator of the soil with horse and plough.

Yiddish. A mixture of Hebrew and **Jerry** spoken by European Jews and those who had immigrated to the East End of London. Yiddish was therefore spoken on both sides of **No Man's Land**. From the German *jüdisch*, Jewish.

'You lot are slower than the second coming of Christ!' The type of sarcasm aimed at recruits by their **drill** instructors. Every **N.C.O.** kept a store of such witticisms to hand. 'You're about as much use as a one-legged man in an arse-kicking contest.' 'You two must be twins – no single person could be so stupid!' 'If brains were shit you'd be constipated!' Etcetera.

'You shouldn't have joined.' The unsympathetic response to anyone complaining of the Army's unfairness.

'You're not paid to think!' The stock retort from an **N.C.O.** to anyone trying to justify his behaviour with a sentence beginning, 'But, I thought . . .' The phrase might also used to rebuff anyone announcing a bright idea.

IS FOR

ZERO

5th West Kent Fusiliers,
British Expeditionary Force,
4th July, 1916.

Dear Edward,

It seems the latest enterprise is turning into
another Loos after all. Our <u>Division</u> has been
<u>put in</u> but not to exploit success. The lads next
door had a terrible time at <u>zero</u> and we have been
sent to stiffen their <u>front</u>. None of the <u>brigades</u>
on our left managed to hold any of their objectives
and ended up exactly where they started. <u>Jerry</u> was
too well dug in. Even where his trenches had been
pulverised he managed to pop up from his <u>dug-</u>
<u>outs</u> as usual. I am told that some <u>battalions</u> were
reaped in swathes, although down south we pushed
him back a decent length and took possession,
so it is not all bad news. The Fifth has lost a few
score from Jerry's counter bombardment but no
names you might know about in 'C' <u>Company</u>.
Our turn will come soon enough.

My wretched ankle is in no hurry to heal. Once
the flood of <u>casualties</u> from the <u>Push</u> has slackened
the <u>M.O.</u> is proposing to send me down to the <u>Base</u>
for an X-ray photograph. In the meantime, he has
rigged me up with a splint and a proper crutch.
It does feel as if my rotten old ankle is broken
again. I might feel less ashamed of myself if I was

properly in _dock_ rather than lying outside on my _valise_, writing drivel like this while an unending stream of _walkers_ heads down _the line_ in bloody bandages. Still, I suppose M & F will be pleased if it all ends in another _Blighty_.

Yours in deepest gloom,

Chazzer . . .

Z-day. The day appointed for the start of a planned attack. Known colloquially as Der Tag, from German, the day. As Z-day grew closer, **staff** officers counted down the last days to it as **X-day** and Y-day.

Zeppelin, Zepp. A **Jerry** airship. From its inventor, Count Zeppelin. During the war, zeppelins came under the command of the German navy not the army. They had an initial impact in terrorising British and French civilians but the **R.F.C.** was eventually able to mount an effective defence.

Zepp in a cloud. A plate of sausage and mash.

Zero, Zero hour. The precise moment, counted down to the second, when synchronised watches showed it was time to attack. In the **artillery**, zero was the moment to open fire. In the **infantry**, it was the moment to **hop the bags**.

Zero in. A series of trial shots to range a rifle or **gun** on its target.

Zig zag. To walk unsteadily when drunk.

Zone call. An urgent appeal to the **artillery** from an observer in a plane calling on all guns within range to hit a particular target with rapid fire. A zone call was expensive in **ammo** and only used if the observer knew for sure that he would be able to destroy a valuable target, such as a large formation of **Jerries** in the open.

Acknowledgements

Every writer approaching the subject of trench lingo is indebted to *Soldier and Sailor Words and Phrases*, by Edward Fraser and John Gibbons (Routledge, 1925) and *The Long Trail*, by John Brophy and Eric Partridge (Scholartis, 1931). For a word collector of the Great War these two sources are the mother lode. That relatively few nuggets from Gibbons, Brophy, *et al*, have made it into *Roger, Sausage & Whippet* suggests how much more verbal treasure lurks out there waiting to be discovered. In carrying out my research for *Roger, Sausage & Whippet* I have been fortunate for the company, on the Western Front and other battlefields, of Andrew Butters, Andrew Craig, Mark Duff, Bill Jackson, Dilip Kaneria and Piers Pool. As far as my wife, Catriona, is concerned, and my two children, Phoebe and Gabriel, I hope that seeing this book in print explains what it is I've been doing in my corner of the bedroom for the past five years.